Mechanical Survival:
the use of reliability data
J. H. Bompas-Smith

Edited by

R. H. W. Brook

London · New York · St Louis · San Francisco · Düsseldorf
Johannesburg · Kuala Lumpur · Mexico · Montreal · New Delhi
Panama · Paris · São Paulo · Singapore · Sydney · Toronto

Published by McGRAW-HILL Book Company (UK) Limited
MAIDENHEAD · BERKSHIRE · ENGLAND

---

07 084411 9

PRINTED AND BOUND IN GREAT BRITAIN

D
620. 0045
BOM

This book is to be returned on or before
the last date stamped below.

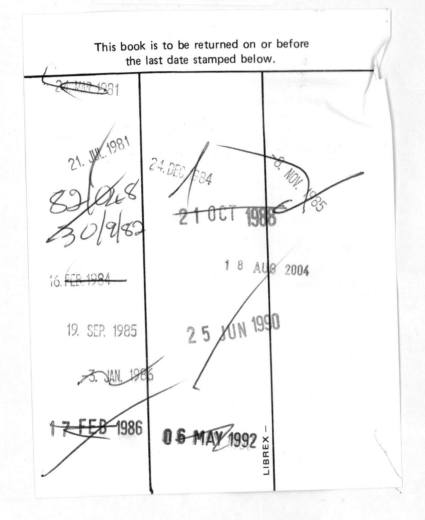

Mechanical survival: the use of reliability data

Contents

	Editor's introduction	vi
Chapter 1	Putting values to reliability	1
Chapter 2	Mortality curves—uses and construction	11
Chapter 3	The special case of constant local failure rate	23
Chapter 4	The theory of failures	27
Chapter 5	The case of increasing failure rate with time when the duty is constant: the normal and log normal distributions	40
Chapter 6	The Weibull, binomial, and Poisson distributions: confidence levels	59
Chapter 7	The initial strength and failure distributions of parts under constant duty: the extreme-value and log extreme-value distributions	85
Chapter 8	Some further considerations regarding distributions of fatigue-test results and minimum fatigue life	99
Chapter 9	The form of the duty distribution	111
Chapter 10	The case where both strength and duty are variables	121
Chapter 11	The effect of 'weak spots'	136
Chapter 12	Mixed distributions	143
Chapter 13	Degradation and replacement curves	150
Chapter 14	The χ^2-distribution, tests for frequency, confidence limits for M.T.B.F.	159
Chapter 15	Simple systems, multiple items, and the effect of maintenance on their reliability	165
Chapter 16	Making the best use of early-failure experience. Pointers from one, two, or three failures	187
Chapter 17	Is reliability a saleable commodity?	193
	Index	197

Editor's introduction

This book was some three parts finished when the untimely death of the author, John Bompas-Smith, prevented his finishing the work. I believe it presents a very valuable contribution to the field of reliability engineering, particularly to those engineers having to deal with things mechanical. It has been my aim to complete and edit the manuscript as far as possible along the lines laid down by the author.

Some very novel ideas are developed herein, all arising from the attractive concept that the patterns of failure of a piece of equipment can be used to diagnose the root cause of failure. The discussions and examples in chapter 11 show by actual examples from real engineering components that this is a very real possibility. When failures develop, the ones that are easy to cure are cured quickly, and the difficult ones are left without a cure. It is these cases where a thorough understanding of the principles of unreliability can help guide the engineer to find the problem he is really trying to solve.

This is not a book that should lie on the Engineering Manager's bookshelf, but should be found in a well-thumbed condition in the Development and Service Engineering general offices.

Engineers are employed to make things work, and they will do that job all the more effectively by understanding the basic principles of why equipment may be unreliable.

R. H. W. Brook

1

Putting values to reliability

Reliability is a word that has existed in our language for a long time but which, in recent years, has taken on an additional meaning. As well as being a purely qualitative noun it is also one that can be quantified. We talk of a reliable car, a reliable make of equipment, or even a reliable person. The question can then be posed 'How reliable?' and this has led, in the case of pieces of equipment, to expressing their reliability in numerical terms. The quantification of reliability has been promoted by the increasing need of extremely reliable and complex pieces of equipment, particularly in the world of space technology, and it is largely because of the needs of the aerospace industry that techniques for ensuring high degrees of reliability have made considerable advances in the last two decades.

As an example of quantification, reliability can be stated as a failure rate, in terms of failures per 1000 hours, or any other convenient unit, or alternatively as the mean time between failures, which is the inverse of the failure rate, being

$$\frac{\text{Total time being considered}}{\text{Number of failures that occur during that time}}.$$

As we shall see shortly, these ways of describing the reliability of a piece of equipment have serious limitations, although they are simple and convenient.

A general definition for the word reliability has been introduced which permits the use of statistical methods and which can be applied universally:

Reliability = the probability that an item will perform satisfactorily for a specified period of time under specified operating conditions.

Different wording may be used but the meaning remains the same. The definition is a general one and some amplification is required when we come to consider particular cases. While time has a definite and understood value both 'perform satisfactorily' and 'operating conditions' are terms which can be interpreted in different ways by different people. These must be clearly defined before reliability can be given a definite value. Take 'perform satisfactorily'. One man may consider his car unsatisfactory if it fails to start at the first press of the button every morning whereas another

1

may be quite content provided it starts at the third or fourth attempt; a third may be unduly worried if his engine has a tendency to overfuel and he sometimes has to wait a minute or two before getting away. Satisfactory is a relative term that must be re-defined for each case that is considered. Only where it is black or white, an item breaks or it does not, is any ambiguity removed.

Operating conditions may be more difficult to define than satisfactory performance. The environmental conditions in which a piece of equipment is going to operate are often not fully known at the time when the equipment is designed or tested, and changes in environment can have a large bearing on the useful lives of some components. There is also the effect of the operating policy of the user.

The word *probability* is associated in statisticians' minds with a value defining the degree of probability in numerical terms and it is in this way that the word is used in the definition of reliability. The use of the word accordingly brings a numerical value into the definition. The degree of probability is usually defined as a decimal fraction of one. A probability of one means absolute certainty, such as the probability that we shall all die some day, whereas a probability of zero indicates absolute impossibility.

When some event occurs, the sum of the probabilities of all the possible outcomes of this event must be one. In the case of a tossed coin, the probability of heads plus the probability of tails $= 0.5 + 0.5 = 1$. Similarly, the probability that an item will perform satisfactorily (be reliable) plus the probability that it will not perform satisfactorily (be unreliable) equals one.

This leads us to the following definition:

$$\text{Unreliability} = \text{the probability that an item will not perform satisfactorily for a specified period of time under specified operating conditions.}$$

The phrases 'perform satisfactorily' and 'not perform satisfactorily' are somewhat cumbersome if they are subject to repetition, so we will use instead the simple terms *survival* and *failure* throughout this book.

The definitions are particularly useful if we are concerned with the likelihood of some equipment completing a particular period of operation. For example, users of military aircraft are interested in the probability that nothing will go wrong with an aircraft despatched on a particular mission, and have devised the term *mission reliability* to describe the probability, the period of time in this instance being the duration of the mission.

Reliability notation

The notation normally used in reliability practice is

R denotes reliability
F denotes unreliability.

2

As we have seen, the sum of these two probabilities is unity, so

$$R + F = 1. \tag{1.1}$$

This equation defines the situation satisfactorily where the equipment concerned has to function only once, for example the firing of a rocket. If, however, the equipment must continue to function over a period of time, its reliability will change with time. Over the time which the equipment is required to operate, the probability of its survival normally decreases as its life increases. It is thus necessary to include in the notation the life for which the reliability figure applies. The normal notation is then

$R(t)$ denotes reliability to time t
$F(t)$ denotes unreliability to time t,

and we can now write

$$R(t) + F(t) = 1. \tag{1.2}$$

Reliability curves

Where unreliability changes with time, as it must do in all cases where any failures are experienced, we can plot a curve of $R(t)$ against t. As an example, Fig. 1.1 shows $R(t)$ against t as applied to the probability of survival of man. Failure, in this case, is defined as death, t is the man's age in years, and $R(t)$ the probability of the man living to the age t. The curve is based on data from the *Registrar-General's Statistical Review of England and Wales 1933* and covers the male deaths that occurred during 1930–32.

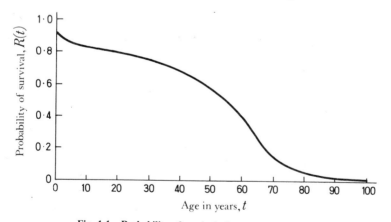

Fig. 1.1   **Probability of survival of a man at any age**

Such a curve is called a *survival curve* and shows the probability of survival of a man to any age. It does not start at 100 per cent because a small percentage of babies die at birth where t is zero. The slope of the curve starts to increase at about 40 years and is steepest between 60 and 70, which is to be expected; it then levels out again because the number of men still surviving becomes small. The prospect of living for over 100 years is remote.

Figure 1.1 may be seen to represent both the probability of survival of an individual man and the proportion of all men in the population that is expected to survive at any given age. Thus $R(t)$ represents both the probability of survival of an individual and the proportion surviving.

If $F(t)$ is plotted against t instead of $R(t)$ the result is simply to turn the survival curve upside down as shown in Fig. 1.2. This is a *mortality curve*, and such curves form the basis of a large proportion of reliability studies.

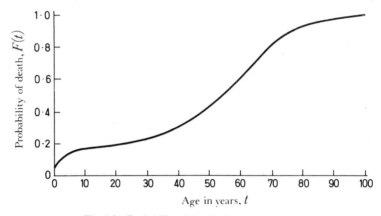

Fig. 1.2   Probability of death of a man at any age

A mortality curve gives values for the proportion of a population that dies, in the case of men, or fail, in the case of components, before a given time. It is thus a cumulative curve, adding up the proportion of the population dying or failing as it rises. In statistical parlance such a curve is called a cumulative probability distribution (C.P.D.).

We will now approach the mortality curve in a different way. If we take a given population, the members of which are now all dead, provided we know their ages at death we can draw a histogram such as the one shown in Fig. 1.3, which shows the same data as that used to draw Figs. 1.1 and 1.2 but set out as a histogram in steps of 5 years. The height of each bar in the histogram represents the number of men's deaths that occurred in the particular 5-year band during the period in which the data was collected. Presentation in histogram form produces a series of steps, but if instead of taking a wide life band, such as 5 years, we progressively reduce the band, the steps get progressively closer together until they disappear and we are left with the continuous curve shown in Fig. 1.4. This form of presentation is known as a probability distribution function (P.D.F.).

4

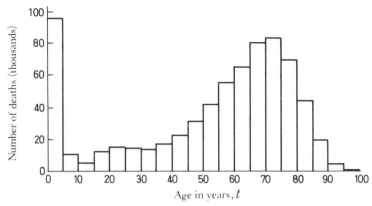

Fig. 1.3   Histogram of number of deaths at various ages

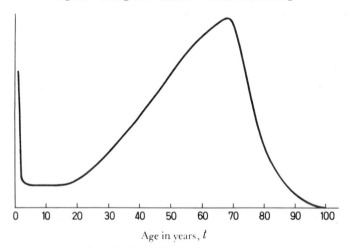

Fig. 1.4   Probability distribution function

Whereas a histogram can be drawn to describe a characteristic of a small number of items, a probability distribution function must embrace a large population. Even if a large population does not actually exist, it must be assumed when we depict a characteristic by means of such a distribution. Reliability theory utilizes distributions to permit the probabilities of survival or failure to be calculated, and clearly we do not always have a large population, such as the men dying in England and Wales during a three-year period, to deal with. We may have say 50 components to consider and at a certain lifetime the distribution may show that the probability of failures is 0·23 equivalent to 11·5 components. Now we cannot have 11·5 failures and this result means that, given a large number of samples of 50 components, we should get an average of 11·5 failures by the lifetime being considered.

5

It will be seen that the vertical scale shown in Fig. 1.3 has been omitted from Fig. 1.4, since the probability-distribution function is a continuous curve, any point on it represents the limiting value of the number of deaths per unit time over a small period as the period tends to zero. We require another method of utilizing it for quantifying probabilities. Now the curve represents the probability of death occurring at all possible ages between birth and extreme longevity and as all men must die the summation of all these probabilities must be certainty. The area under the curve is accordingly equal to unity. The probability of death up to a given age can be obtained by integrating the curve between zero and that age, or the probability of death between certain ages by integrating between these ages.

Provided we know the probability-distribution function, we can derive the mortality curve by continuous integration. If the probability-distribution function is described mathematically by $f(t)$, then

$$F(t) = \int_0^t f(t) \, dt. \qquad (1.3)$$

It follows that, where the mortality curve is known, we can find the probability distribution function by differentiation:

$$f(t) = \frac{dF(t)}{dt}. \qquad (1.4)$$

Failure rate

When we talk about failure rate we mean the

$$\frac{\text{Number of failures}}{\text{Length of time during which failures can occur}},$$

and we usually express this in terms of failures per hour or some multiple of hours such as a thousand. Instead of hours we may use number of operations or cycles. Values of the failure rate derived in this way can be very misleading, because the failure rate may change appreciably with the life of the equipment being considered, as we saw in the case of human life. To take another example, suppose we drive a series of wooden fence posts into the ground. The failure rate will be zero for a number of years, then the posts will start to rot, and taking the time from which the rot sets in the failure rate per year will be appreciable. A large range of equipment behaves in the same way so that we usually require to know, not only the overall failure rate, but the failure rate during any particular period of life.

The simplest way of stating this is in terms of the failure rate per unit time at any given lifetime.

$$\frac{\text{The failure rate}}{\text{per unit time}} = \frac{\begin{array}{c}\text{Number of failures we expect during a unit of time at a} \\ \text{given lifetime}\end{array}}{\text{Number of items exposed to failure at the same lifetime}}$$

This is given the symbol $Z(t)$ where t is the lifetime being considered.

A special cases arises where $Z(t)$ remains constant, that is, the failure rate does not change with the life of the equipment. This state of affairs occurs when the failures are due to accidental causes that can happen at any time, such as birds striking aircraft or a car tyre picking up a nail on the road.

Where the failure rate remains constant it has become common practice to denote it by the symbol λ instead of $Z(t)$.

A number of different names have been given to $Z(t)$ and λ in the literature on reliability. They have been called the *hazard rate*, being the rate of hazard to the equipment, or *force of mortality* which is also a reasonable definition. Another name sometimes met with is *instantaneous failure rate* but this is really a contradiction in terms since any rate must have a finite denominator. The name that is gaining in popularity and which we shall use in this book is *local failure rate*, which is an unambiguous definition.

Relationship between $R(t)$, $F(t)$, $f(t)$ and $Z(t)$

Consider Fig. 1.5, which shows a probability-distribution function $f(t)$ and the proportion surviving at time t, $R(t)$. Between t and $t + 1$ the proportion expected to fail is

$$\int_{t}^{t+1} f(t)\, dt,$$

and since the proportion $R(t)$ is surviving, the local failure rate by definition is given by

$$Z(t) = \frac{\int_{t}^{t+1} f(t)\, dt}{R(t)} = \frac{f(t)}{R(t)}. \tag{1.5}$$

It will be seen that $\int_{t}^{t+1} f(t)\, dt = f(t)$ if dt is equal to 1 and the height of the curve is assumed to be height $f(t)$ between t and $t + 1$.

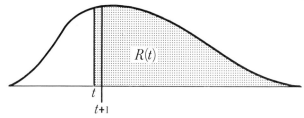

$R(t)$

t

$t+1$

Fig. 1.5 Derivation of local failure rate

7

We can combine eqs. (1.2) and (1.5) and write

$$Z(t) = \frac{f(t)}{1 - F(t)} \qquad (1.6)$$

and including eq. (1.4) write

$$Z(t) = \frac{dF(t)/dt}{1 - F(t)}, \qquad (1.7)$$

so that $Z(t)$ is seen to be a function of the mortality curve. The curve of $Z(t)$ derived from the previous curves is shown in Fig. 1.6.

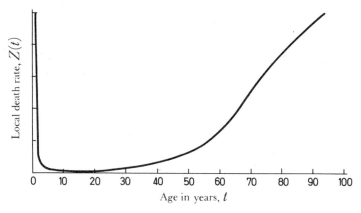

Fig. 1.6   Local death rate v age

We will now examine the relationship between $R(t)$ and $Z(t)$:

$$Z(t) = \frac{f(t)}{R(t)} = \frac{dF(t)}{dt} \frac{1}{R(t)}$$

$$\therefore \int_0^t Z(t)\, dt = \int_0^t \frac{dF(t)}{dt} \frac{dt}{R(t)} = \int_{F(0)}^{F(t)} \frac{dF(t)}{1 - F(t)}$$

$$= [-\log_e(1 - F(t))]_{F(0)}^{F(t)} = [-\log_e R(t)]_0^t$$

$$= -\log_e R(t) \quad \text{(at zero time } F(0) = 0)$$

$$\therefore R(0) = 1, \log_e R(0) = 0$$

Hence,

$$R(t) = \exp\left(- \int_0^t Z(t)\, dt\right), \qquad (1.8)$$

and from eq. (1.5),

$$f(t) = Z(t) \exp\left(- \int_0^t Z(t)\, dt\right). \qquad (1.9)$$

8

Defining distributions

When we use the term distribution, we simply mean the probability distribution, which can be described by either the cumulative probability distribution or the probability distribution function. A mortality curve is a distribution of failures expressed as the cumulative probability distribution.

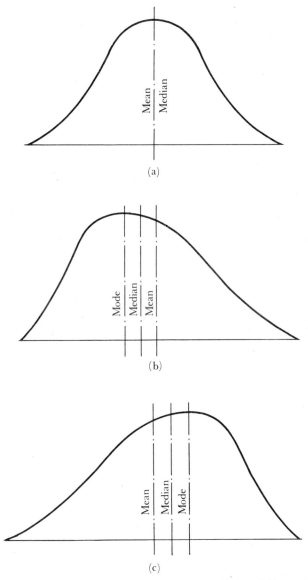

Fig. 1.7 Basic distribution shapes : (a) symmetrical, (b) positively skewed, (c) negatively skewed

There is an infinite number of different forms or shapes that distributions associated with reliability can follow, and during our studies we shall see that many of these shapes can be described by mathematical expressions, and also how they are determined by the various engineering parameters that control a particular situation.

There is a number of terms used in connection with distributions and these should be understood. A distribution that is symmetrically disposed about a mid-point is called a *symmetrical* distribution, and one that is biased in one direction a *skew* distribution. Bias to the left is defined as positively skewed and to the right as negatively skewed (see Fig. 1.7).

The average of the values of all the observations that go to make up the distribution is called the *mean*. For a symmetrical distribution, the mean lies at the mid-point of a symmetrical distribution, but for a skewed distribution it will move in the direction of the tail.

The middle value is called the *median*, that is, the value for which half the observations are lower and half higher. The median accordingly corresponds to the value at which there is a 50 per cent probability, as half the area of the distribution lies on either side of it.

In a symmetrical distribution the mean and median coincide at the central value, whereas for skew distribution they are different (see Fig. 1.7). Another term is the *mode*, which is the value at which the largest number of observations occur, that is, at which the maximum height of the distribution is reached.

Most distributions that arise in reliability practice are skewed and it is important to realize that, in this case, the average life to failure as given by the mean is not the same as the life at which there is a 50 per cent probability of failure, the median life.

2

Mortality curves—uses and construction

The mortality curves of engineering components follow the same general form as that experienced by human beings. We can expect some initial failures due to manufacturing faults that become apparent as soon as the equipment is put into use—anyone who takes delivery of a new car almost invariably finds a few faults that have to be rectified. There then follows a period of useful life, during which time there are few failures and those that do occur are isolated random occurrences; this part of the curve corresponds to the part of the human mortality curve between the high infant mortality rate and the onset of old age, during which death is normally due to accidental causes or the contraction of a disease which occurs by mischance and is independent of age. The local failure rate during this period is constant. The final portion of the curve reflects the old-age phase, or wear-out as it is usually termed in the case of engineering components.

Writers on reliability have frequently taken the curve of $Z(t)$ against t, tidied it up so as to define these three phases clearly and called it the 'bathtub' curve. An example is shown in Fig. 2.1. This curve presents a useful concept, but as may be expected there are considerable differences between the $Z(t)$ against t curves actually experienced.

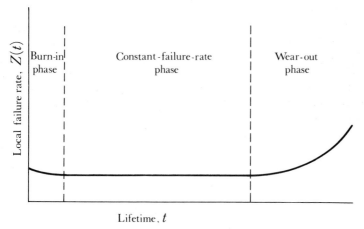

Fig. 2.1   **Bathtub curve**

In engineering practice we are seldom able to draw a complete mortality curve as we can only do this where many components are allowed to continue their life until they fail, a situation that is normally unacceptable. We may have a number of test results which tell us the form in the middle of the curve but not much about the important beginning where the earliest failures may occur. Alternatively, we may have data from service experience, in which case we shall be able to draw the portion of the curve that covers the early and constant-failure-rate regions and in some cases the beginning of the wear-out phase.

We shall shortly study methods of calculating mortality curves and in the succeeding chapters we shall study their form and the way that this derives from engineering and material-strength considerations.

In order that the reader will not feel that these studies are merely an academic exercise but will see how they provide him with a tool for problem solving and decision making, we will briefly review some of their more important uses.

Some uses of mortality curves

Two of the most important uses of mortality curves involve extrapolation, upwards and downwards. We shall study later how such extrapolation can be performed in a satisfactory way by fitting the curve to a suitable statistical distribution of known form.

Prediction of future failures This is an obvious use of a mortality curve where only the lower portion is known, and it is achieved by extrapolating the curve upwards.

Prediction of life to first failure of a large population A mortality curve is often drawn from data that relates to experience from a small sample. If we wish to know the lifetime that we expect a part to achieve before any failures occur when a large population of parts is involved, we must extrapolate the curve downwards. Since the mortality curve becomes asymptotic with the horizontal axis it is not possible to establish a life for no failures, but we can estimate a life where the probability of failure is acceptably remote. The lifetime value obtained in this way provides a datum from which the degree of improvement required can be gauged.

The method is particularly useful where tests to failure are carried out on a small number of samples. Even if all of these fail at lifetime greater than required by the specification, the variation in lifetime to failure may show that some failures will occur before the specified life.

Estimation of economic life or maintenance For this we do not use the mortality curve directly, but the curve of $Z(t)$ which can be derived from it.

Multiplying the values of $Z(t)$ by the cost of the failure provides us with a curve of failure cost per hour against life. This curve can be added to a curve of the cost of replacement, additional maintenance or cost of modification to assess the economics of taking action. An example is shown in Fig. 2.2, which relates to the economics of replacing a gear that was prone to failure. The lines showing cost of failure and cost of replacement in terms of cost per hour have been added together to produce the total cost line. This latter is a shallow curve which shows the life band during which replacement is desirable.

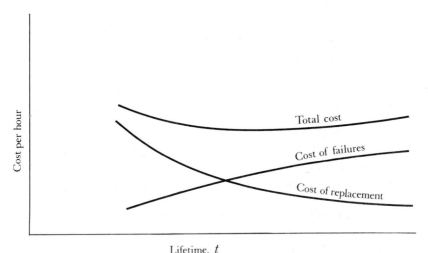

Fig. 2.2

Indication of more than one mode or cause of failure   An engineer presented with some severely damaged remains may be unable to determine the exact mode or cause of the failure. He will assess the cause as best he can and take action to put matters right. Now, if there are actually two causes of the failure, he will be disappointed to find that the failures still persist; even if his diagnosis and cure were right they will only have dealt with part of the problem.

A mortality curve gives an indication of the presence of two modes or causes of failure because one of the modes normally starts before the other and this produces a kink in the curve at the time that the second mode starts to occur. Mortality curves plotted on linear scales do not show this kink very clearly but we shall see that other forms of plotting provide a clear indication of more than one mode or cause of failure.

Information about variability   From the mortality curve it is a simple matter to estimate the variation that exists in the life to failure. We thus

13

have information about variability that can be used in a number of ways, such as:

(a) To show the possibility of eliminating failures by reducing the variability rather than strengthening the component
(b) Where the amount of variability is greater than would be expected from engineering considerations there is an indication that some additional factor, such as variable quality, is influencing the failures
(c) By assessing the variability of lives to failure in relation to different operating parameters, it is possible to estimate the relative effects of these parameters.

Calculating mortality curves

We will now examine the ways that are open to us of calculating the points on the curve. These ways assume a knowledge of both the lifetime at which failures occurred and the number of items exposed to failure at that life-time, data without which mortality curves cannot be drawn.

While the definition of reliability refers to a single item, a sample of one is clearly insufficient evidence from which to draw a mortality curve. The larger the sample the more accurate our assessment will be. Five instances of unsatisfactory performance or failures can be regarded as a minimum sample size and we shall see later how confidence in our assessment increases when a large number of failures is taken into account.

To draw a curve, we need to calculate the probability of failure at various lifetimes. Two ways of doing this are open to us, proportion or ranking. Proportion methods are applicable only to field failures where a large number of items have been exposed to failure.

Calculation using proportion   Let us consider N items which fail in turn at lives $t_1, t_2, \ldots, t_N$. Then, the probability of failure at lifetime t_1 can be approximated by

$$F(t_1) = 1/N;$$

at lifetime t_2 by

$$F(t_2) = 2/N,$$

and at lifetime t_N by

$$F(t_N) = N/N = 1,$$

which means total unreliability. In general, we have

$$F(t_n) = \frac{n}{N}, \tag{2.1}$$

where t_n is the time of the nth failure out of a total number N exposed to failure *provided that all the N items were equally exposed to failure.*

This simple equation is reasonable in so far as the particular N items are concerned, but if the N items are regarded as a sample of a larger population, it is easy to see that it falls down at the high values of $F(t)$. This is so because although the last survivor in the sample fails at t_N, it is unlikely that this would be the strongest member of the whole population, and so t_N cannot be regarded as the lifetime at which all items would have failed. The same objection does not apply to low values of $F(t)$, and the equation provides a simple means of calculating the reliability where all items have not failed. For this reason, the proportion method is not suitable for use when plotting test results where all items on tests proceeded to failure. In these circumstances ranking should be used.

Equation (2.1) is applicable where all the items concerned continue to failure, a condition that is clearly true in the case of a test on light bulbs which are connected in parallel and all switched on simultaneously, none of the bulbs being removed prior to failure. For many test results and field results, some items are taken out of use for reasons other than failures, affecting the numbers exposed to failures at different lifetimes, and a correction to take this into account must be included in the calculation.

Method I—From first principles. Suppose that we have a number of items that have been put into use and that failure occurs at lives of $t_1, t_2, t_3, \ldots$, the number of failures occurring at each lifetime being n_1, n_2, n_3, and the number of items actually exposed to failure at each lifetime being $N_1, N_2, N_3, \ldots$.

At t_1 the proportion expected to fail is n_1/N_1, and this gives us our first point on the curve. We now calculate the number that would have failed at t_2, provided the original number (N_1) had been allowed to proceed to failure.

Since n_1 failed at t_1, the original number has been reduced to $N_1 - n_1$. The proportion actually failing at t_2 is n_2/N_2, so the number that would have failed had N_1 proceeded to failure is

$$(N_1 - n_1)\frac{n_2}{N_2},$$

and the proportion of N_1 expected to fail at t_2 is

$$(N_1 - n_1)\frac{n_2}{N_2 N_1}.$$

We now proceed to estimate the proportion of N_1 that would fail at t_3 in the same way.

If the original number had been allowed to proceed to failure, the number

15

exposed to failure at t_3 would be

$$N_1 - \left[n_1 + (N_1 - n_1) \frac{n_2}{N_2} \right],$$

and the proportion of N_1 expected to fail at t_3 is

$$N_1 - \left[n_1 + (N_1 - n_1) \frac{n_2}{N_2} \right] \frac{n_3}{N_1 N_3}.$$

The same process can be repeated for subsequent values. To obtain the value of $F(t)$ for a given value of t it is necessary only to sum the proportions of N_1 expected to fail up to the required value of t.

While the calculation may appear somewhat complicated when set out algebraically, it is in fact very simple when set out in a tabulated form, and an example of this is shown in Table 2.1.

Table 2.1   Calculation of points on the mortality curve by proportion method from first principles

(1)	(2)	(3)	(4)	(5)	(6)	(7)
Lifetime to failure in hours	Number of failures	Number exposed to failure	Number of failures expected if all original population had been allowed to proceed to failure	Cumulative number of failures expected	F(t)	R(t)
141	1	202	$1 \cdot 0$	$1 \cdot 0$	0·0049	0·9951
337	1	177	$1 \times \dfrac{202 - 1}{177} = 1 \cdot 135$	2·135	0·0106	0·9894
364	1	176	$1 \times \dfrac{202 - 2 \cdot 135}{176} = 1 \cdot 135$	3·27	0·0162	0·9838
542	1	165	$1 \times \dfrac{202 - 3 \cdot 27}{165} = 1 \cdot 20$	4·47	0·0221	0·9779
716	1	156	$1 \times \dfrac{202 - 4 \cdot 47}{156} = 1 \cdot 27$	5·74	0·0284	0·9716
765	1	153	$1 \times \dfrac{202 - 5 \cdot 74}{153} = 1 \cdot 28$	7·02	0·0347	0·9613
940	1	144	$1 \times \dfrac{202 - 7 \cdot 02}{144} = 1 \cdot 35$	8·37	0·0414	0·9586
986	1	143	$1 \times \dfrac{202 - 8 \cdot 37}{143} = 1 \cdot 35$	9·72	0·0481	0·9519

The example used relates to actual failures of bearings experienced in customer use. Columns (1), (2), and (3) give the data on which the calculation is based, the life to failure (column 1) being arranged in ascending order. Column 4 shows the number of failures expected if all the original population, in this case 202, had been allowed to proceed to failure, and in column 5 this number is accumulated. The accumulated numbers from column 5 are fed back into the calculation carried out in the next line of column 4. The final stage is to divide the figures in column 5 by the original number N_1 (202), thus obtaining values for $F(t)$ (column 6). We can find $R(t)$, if required, by subtracting $F(t)$ from unity.

The mortality curve $F(t)$ calculated in Table 2.1 is shown plotted in Fig. 2.3. It is only a small part of the whole curve, in fact it only goes up to $F(t) = 0.048$. It is representative of the portion of the curve that can be drawn from data obtained when an item is in customer use and early wear-out failures are experienced.

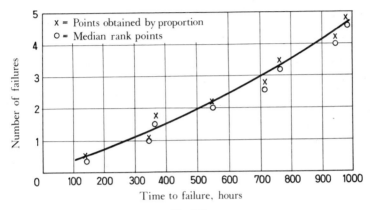

Fig. 2.3

The mortality curve as calculated is seen to be a series of steps; a failure occurs which increases the cumulative proportion failed, after which there is a period of no failures and the reliability remains constant. These steps occur because we are drawing a curve representative of a relatively small population; if we had an infinite population, so that we had failures at small lifetime increments, the steps would clearly disappear. It is thus quite in order to draw a curve through the plotted points.

In the last example the actual lives to failure were used. In practice, however, it is sometimes difficult to obtain exact data, or alternatively we may have a large number of failures, so that the calculation is rather long. In such cases, we can combine groups of failures that occur at similar lifetimes into lifetime bands, and calculate the mortality for lifetime bands rather than exact lifetimes. The exposure should be taken as

$$\frac{\text{(Total hours of all good components in the lifetime band}}{\text{Width of lifetime band in hours}},$$

and the probability of failure and unreliability is considered to apply to the middle of the lifetime band.

17

Method II—Using the product rule. It can be shown that

$$R(t_N) = R(t_1)R(t_2)R(t_3)\ldots R(t_n), \tag{2.2}$$

where $t_1, t_2, t_3, \ldots, t_n$ are increments of time with sum t_N, and $R(t_1)$, $R(t_2)$, etc. represent the proportion surviving during these time increments which are given by

$$1 - \frac{\text{Number of failures during increment}}{\text{Number exposed to failure during increment}}.$$

We shall see the proof of this statement when we consider the product rule in chapter 15.

At time increments where there are no failures $R = 1$, so it is in order to take $R(t_1)$, $R(t_2)$, etc. as the points in time at which failures actually occur. Alternatively, lifetime bands can be used as explained previously.

This method gives exactly the same result as method I but the calculation is somewhat simpler and it is accordingly to be preferred. The tabulation is given in Table 2.2 using the same data as for the previous tabulation. The proportion failing is calculated in column 4 and this is then converted into the proportion surviving, column 5, by subtracting from unity. The cumulative probability of survival, $R(t)$, column 6, is obtained by multiplying together the figures in column 5, and finally the probability of failure $F(t)$ is found by subtracting the values in column 6 from unity.

Table 2.2 Calculation of points on the mortality curve by proportion method using the product rule

(1)	(2)	(3)	(4)	(5)	(6)	(7)
Lifetime to failure in hours	Number of failures	Number exposed to failure	Proportion failed	Proportion survived	$R(t)$	$F(t)$
141	1	202	$\frac{1}{202} = 0\cdot00495$	0·99505	0·9951	0·0049
337	1	177	$\frac{1}{177} = 0\cdot00565$	0·99435	0·9894	0·0106
364	1	176	$\frac{1}{176} = 0\cdot00568$	0·99432	0·9838	0·0162
542	1	165	$\frac{1}{165} = 0\cdot06606$	0·99394	0·9779	0·0221
716	1	156	$\frac{1}{156} = 0\cdot00641$	0·99346	0·9716	0·0284
765	1	153	$\frac{1}{153} = 0\cdot00654$	0·99346	0·9613	0·0347
940	1	144	$\frac{1}{144} = 0\cdot00694$	0·99306	0·9586	0·0414
986	1	143	$\frac{1}{143} = 0\cdot00699$	0·99301	0·9519	0·0481

Calculation using ranking When we have a case where all the parts concerned fail, such as when a number of parts are tested to failure, the best method of drawing the curve is by a process known as *ranking*.

To explain the principle of ranking we will take the very simple example of three parts that are tested to failure. In practice such a test would be valueless for curve-plotting purposes but this need not detract from its use as an example. We wish to estimate the best values on the probability scale against which to plot the times to failure.

The situation is illustrated in Fig. 2.4, which shows a hypothetical distribution of times to failure for a large number of parts tested to failure. The distributions of times of the 1st, 2nd, and 3rd failures that would result if a considerable number of samples of three were tested in the same way have been derived from it and are also shown.

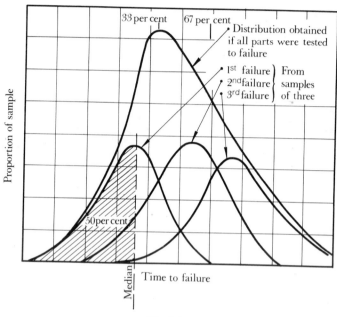

Fig. 2.4

If we had used proportion methods to plot our three failures we should have plotted the first failure at 33 per cent. This would clearly be incorrect as reference to Fig. 2.4 will show; the 33 per cent and 67 per cent lines for the overall distribution are marked at the top of the figure.

We must clearly plot our three original failure points at the most appropriate point of the distributions of 1st, 2nd, and 3rd failures. In the case of each failure there is a 50 per cent chance that the failure will occur before the median life of the relevant distribution and 50 per cent that it will occur after it. The best estimate that we can make of the time to failure is to take the median life. If we repeated our test with a number of samples of three, and took the average life to failure of the first failures, we should plot the result at the probability corresponding to the mean value for each of the three distributions. If we take the results of a test on three parts, the

19

best estimates of the probabilities of failure are the medians of the individual distributions, which can be shown to be equivalent to 20 per cent, 50 per cent, and 80 per cent of the overall distributions.

We have now carried out the process of ranking, which is simply to allocate the most likely level of probability to each failure. We define the order in which the failures occur, or in which they would occur if all the components failed, as the *rank order number*, and the probability associated with the median of the distributions for each rank order number as the *median rank*. We shall see later how the values of the median ranks are calculated.

A very good approximation can be obtained from the expression

$$\text{Median rank} = \frac{J - 0\cdot3}{N + 0\cdot4}, \tag{2.3}$$

where J is the rank order number,

N is the number originally exposed to failure.

An alternative method that is frequently used is to calculate the rank values from $J/(N + 1)$. This gives a value that lies between the median and the mean, and has the virtue of being easy to calculate. As N increases, the difference between the rank value obtained in this way and the median rank becomes small.

It would be invidious to argue the relative merits of the two alternatives, because in practice the errors that arise due to the particular sample that is tested or exposed to failure are much greater than any differences due to the alternative methods of calculating the rank values.

Ranking and proportion methods compared   We have shown that, for a sample of three items tested to failure, proportion methods for calculating the curve are valueless. If instead of three we had a larger number exposed to failure N, any error due to using proportion methods would become correspondingly less. For example, when $N = 50$, the median rank for the first failure is 1·38 per cent which can be compared with the proportion of 2 per cent.

We see that proportion methods are satisfactory when we have large numbers exposed to failure but that where the numbers are small or we require to plot complete sets of data, for example test results, ranking must be used.

Ranking methods where all items do not proceed to failure   When we have data similar to that given in the earlier example, where not all items have not proceeded to failure, either because they are still in operation or because they have been taken out of use for other reasons, we can still use the ranking method.

To calculate the median rank value we require to know the rank number of the failure, and where some items do not proceed to failure we must make allowance for them in the same way as we did when we carried out our calculation from first principles. Referring to Table 2.1, it will be seen that the figures in column 5 are actually the rank order numbers we require, and we can proceed to calculate the median rank values. The tabulation is set out in Table 2.3 and the resulting points plotted in Fig. 2.3.

As expected, the ranking method gives a rather lower probability of failure than the proportion method, and statistically it is to be preferred.

Table 2.3 Calculation of points on the mortality curve using ranking

(1)	(2)	(3)	(4)	(5)	(6)	(7)
Lifetime to failure in hours	Number of failures	Number exposed to failure	Number of failures expected if all the original population had been allowed to proceed to failure	Rank order number	Ranks (per cent)	
					Median	$\dfrac{n}{N+1}$
141	1	202	1.0	1.0	0.346	0.493
337	1	177	$1 \times \dfrac{202 - 1}{177} = 1.135$	2.135	0.907	1.052
364	1	176	$1 \times \dfrac{202 - 2.13}{176} = 1.135$	3.27	1.467	1.611
542	1	165	$1 \times \dfrac{202 - 3.26}{165} = 1.20$	4.47	2.060	2.202
716	1	156	$1 \times \dfrac{202 - 4.46}{156} = 1.27$	5.74	2.638	2.827
765	1	153	$1 \times \dfrac{202 - 5.73}{153} = 1.28$	7.02	3.320	3.458
940	1	144	$1 \times \dfrac{202 - 7.01}{144} = 1.35$	8.37	3.987	4.123
986	1	143	$1 \times \dfrac{202 - 8.36}{143} = 1.35$	9.72	4.654	4.788

How accurate are mortality curves? It is appropriate to conclude this chapter with an account of a simple exercise carried out by the author, which demonstrates how discretion must be used in drawing conclusions from mortality curves where a small number of components are subjected to test.

For this exercise a typical mortality curve was assumed. It was divided into 100 sections of equal probability so that each section represented one failure out of 100. The times to each failure were then read off the curve and entered on to small pieces of paper, these were well shuffled and three samples of 20 drawn at random from the file. The pieces of paper can be regarded as 20 components, selected at random and tested to failure. The resultant mortality curves are shown in Fig. 2.5; they show the same general pattern but also the considerable differences that can arise due to the selection of samples. The results obtained show a nearly two to one difference in life for 10 per cent failures.

In a later chapter we shall study how to surround a mortality curve with a band within which the curve will lie with a known degree of probability.

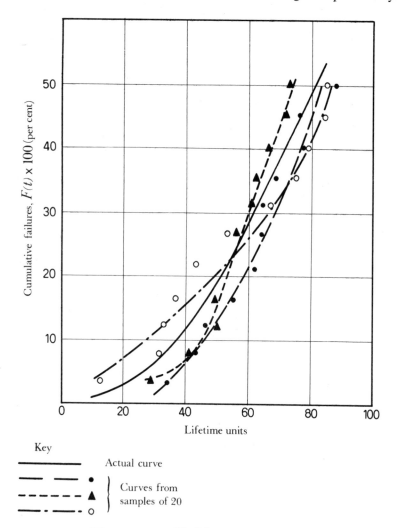

Fig. 2.5

3

The special case of constant local failure rate

We have seen that a constant local failure rate can apply during a period of the useful life of a component. This constant rate occurs more frequently in the case of electronic than mechanical components. We shall meet examples later where a nearly constant local failure applies to wear-out failures, due to special circumstances, in addition to random and non-time related failures.

Where we are concerned with the overall failure rate of a large number of similar components with different lifetimes, it is usual to treat this rate as constant and take the overall rate as the average rate for the components, some of which are new and have a low rate, and others are older and have a higher rate. The average rate is the most valuable figure for many practical purposes.

The special case of a constant local failure rate has accordingly an important place in reliability theory.

The mathematics associated with it are simple and the data required for its computation minimal. This has produced a tendency to assume a constant failure rate in cases where there has been little or no logical reason for such an assumption. Unless it can be demonstrated that a constant failure exists, or the problem concerns the overall failure rate, where the lifetimes of the components vary, simple solutions offered by the assumption of a constant rate should be excluded.

The mathematics of the constant failure rate

We start with eq. (1.8):

$$R(t) = e\left(-\int_0^t Z(t)\,dt\right).$$

Substituting λ, the constant local failure rate, for $Z(t)$, and integrating, we have

$$R(t) = e^{-\lambda t}. \tag{3.1}$$

23

We can then say that, from eq. (1.2),

$$F(t) = 1 - e^{-\lambda t}. \tag{3.2}$$

From eq. (1.4),

$$f(t) = \frac{\mathrm{d}F(t)}{\mathrm{d}t} = \lambda\, e^{-\lambda t}. \tag{3.3}$$

If the assumption is made that the local failure rate remains constant, its value can be calculated very easily by

$$\lambda = \frac{\text{Number of failures}}{\text{Number of time units during which all items were exposed to failure}}.$$

Instead of λ, its inverse, *mean time between failures* or M.T.B.F. is often used, and denoted by the symbol m:

$$\frac{1}{\lambda} = m$$

$$= \frac{\text{Number of time units during which all items were exposed to failure}}{\text{Number of failures}}.$$

In terms of m, the reliability is expressed by

$$R(t) = e^{-t/m}. \tag{3.4}$$

The equation $R(t) = e^{-\lambda t}$ describes a probability distribution known as the *negative exponential distribution*. An example of the cumulative probability distribution, which is a plot of the values for $R(t)$ against the

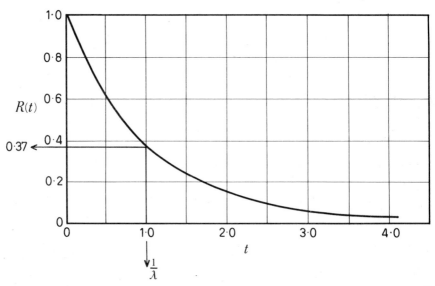

Fig. 3.1

24

variable t, is shown in Fig. 3.1. A point to be noted is the value of $R(t)$, where t is equal to the mean time between failures, m or $1/\lambda$. This value is 0·37, so that $F(t) = 0·63$, which is the average time to failure or characteristic life. It should be noted that the M.T.B.F. and the characteristic life are not equal except in the constant failure rate case. Plotting $F(t)$ against t clearly produces the same curve the other way up.

The probability distribution function $f(t)$ has the same form as $R(t)$ since it is given by $\lambda e^{-\lambda t}$.

A check for the presence of a constant failure rate

Having calculated the points for a mortality curve, we may wish to check whether the curve conforms to the constant failure rate case. The equation for $F(t)$ can be treated as follows:

$$F(t) = 1 - e^{-\lambda t}$$

$$1 - F(t) = e^{-\lambda t}$$

$$\frac{1}{1 - F(t)} = e^{\lambda t}$$

$$\log_e \frac{1}{1 - F(t)} = \lambda t. \tag{3.5}$$

Accordingly, if $1/[1 - F(t)]$ is plotted on a log scale against t on a linear scale we shall get a straight line of slope λ if a constant failure rate is applicable.

It may be noted that, when $t = m = 1/\lambda$, we have

$$F(t) = 0·63 \quad \text{and} \quad \log_e \frac{1}{1 - F(t)} = 1$$

This provides us with a graphical means for estimating the mean time between failures.

A good approximation for $1 - e^{-\lambda t}$

The use of $e^{-\lambda t}$, while theoretically correct, introduces a complication into the mathematics of reliability which is frequently quite unnecessary for practical purposes.

How many engineers, when told that one failure had occurred in a 1000 hour trial would not say that the chance of a failure in a 10 hour trial would be 0·01? In fact we know that it is $1 - e^{-0·01}$, but working this out still gives 0·01.

25

We see that λt can be a good approximation to $1 - e^{-\lambda t}$. This approximation is very good down to $\lambda t = 0.05$, and often good enough for practical purposes down to $\lambda t = 0.10$, after which $1 - e^{-\lambda t}$ must be used.

The reader can easily check this by reference to a table of negative exponential values.

4

The theory of failures

The derivation of failure distributions

Failures occur when the strength of a component and the load or duty imposed on it become incompatible. To take a simple example, consider the case of an item that is only required to function once, and assume that both the strength of the item and the duty it has to perform are subject to variation, an assumption that is always true to some extent. Now if the weakest item can endure the most severe duty without failing, it will be completely reliable—if not, failures are to be expected.

Variations in strength and duty can be described by means of probability distributions which may or may not conform to one of the statistical probability distributions that can be defined mathematically. We shall call the probability distribution defining the variations in strength the strength distribution and that defining the variations in duty the duty distribution.

Strength is definable as the strength of the material, though as we shall see, a number of different material properties may be involved if it is considered relative to the time to failure. The surface condition of the material also affects the initial strength if fatigue or corrosion are the cause of failure. Dimensional variations must be treated as affecting variability of duty rather than the variability of strength, since they affect the stress imposed on the part and not the material strength.

The situation that arises when the strength and duty distributions overlap is represented in Fig. 4.1, which relates to a particular example of an item that is required to function only once, match sticks. Some boxes of matches contain match sticks that are rather thin and others do not have a straight grain. Their strength is variable. Since the majority are usually quite good matches their strength has been represented by a narrow band, the good matches, and a tail, the poor ones.

The duty is the force that is used to strike them. Failures will occur if one of the matches in the area of overlap is unfortunate enough to encounter a degree of duty greater than its strength will withstand and the probability of failures is obtained by integrating the product of the values of the two probabilities over the length of the overlap.

Most components have to continue functioning for a period of time, and

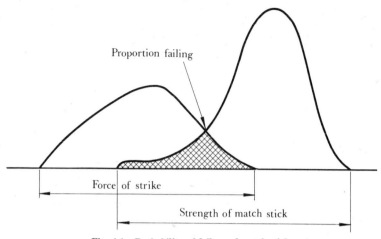

Fig. 4.1   Probability of failure of match sticks

this brings in a third variable, time or number of cycles. In the majority of cases the duty remains the same, except for its normal scatter, irrespective of time. On the other hand, the strength frequently changes with time. Strength can be reduced by wear, corrosion or chemical attack, metal fatigue and many other causes, all of which take time to become effective.

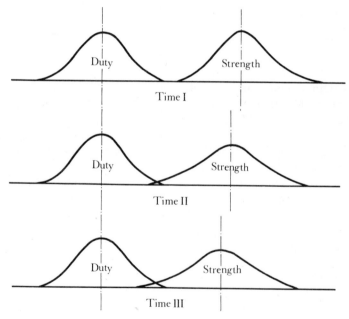

Fig. 4.2   Probability of failures related to time

This reduction in strength with time both changes the mean and increases the spread of the strength distribution.

In Fig. 4.2, this is illustrated by a series of diagrams showing the relationship between the duty and strength distributions, the duty distribution being the same in each case and the strength distribution both moving towards it and increasing its spread with the passage of time. The time at which failures start to occur is clearly dependent on the strength/time relationship involved. This relationship is often related to the level of duty,

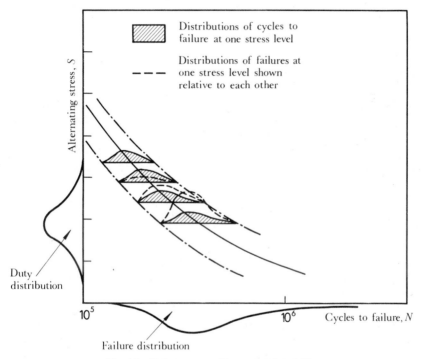

Fig. 4.3   Fatigue curve with associated variables

as in the case of deterioration due to creep and fatigue. Since we are dealing with failures, we are concerned with the combined duty/time-to-failure relationship. Provided this relationship is known, the diagram shown in Fig. 4.2 can be taken a stage further, as is done in Fig. 4.3, which shows part of a stress/cycles-to-failure fatigue curve for mild steel. The fatigue strength of a material is represented by the distributions drawn round the mean curve at various stress levels, these being the strength distribution at different levels of duty. A possible distribution of duty is shown on the left of the diagram.

If we consider an increment of the duty distribution, corresponding to a specific level of duty or stress, the proportion of components lying in this increment can be expected to fail according to the fatigue-strength distribution at the specific stress level. The dotted distributions in Fig. 4.3 represent failures at different stress levels, the areas being in proportion to the equivalent increments of the duty distribution.

These distributions of failures can be added together and this sum will represent the distribution of the failures for the whole population, or following the previous terminology, the failure distribution. This is shown under the horizontal ordinate. In the simple case, where the duty remains constant at all times, and over all the components being considered, the duty distribution disappears and the failure distribution is equal to the strength distribution at the applicable level of duty. This simple state of affairs is rarely found in practice except where equipment is tested under controlled laboratory conditions. With equipment in customer service, differences in use pattern, environment, or maintenance lead to differences in the level of duty imposed. The form of failure distributions that arise from equipment in customer use must accordingly be expected to be affected by a duty distribution.

Clearly, the greater the spread of the duty distribution, the greater the spread of the failure distribution. There are exceptions to this rule where there is a limiting duty below which no failure will occur, such as with fatigue in hard materials, but this does not alter our general argument.

We can sum up by saying that the form and spread of the failure distribution is dependent on

(a) The form and spread of the duty distribution
(b) The form and spread of the strength distribution
(c) The form of the duty/time-to-failure relationship.

This concept requires some modification where the failure results from more than one process. For example, a part may be weakened by corrosion until it reaches a stage where the load is so high that it fails. There is no connection between the corrosive influence and the load, but both are variable and the particular value of each factor influences the time to failure.

The diagram in Fig. 4.3 is applicable only to cases where the degrading mechanism is associated with application of stress, such as fatigue and creep. Where the degrading mechanism is wear, corrosion, or some other mechanism not associated with the loading of the part, the diagram becomes complicated by the introduction of a second duty distribution. We will look at this complication later, and confine our immediate objective to an examination of the ways in which a part degrades and the relationship between the time to degrade to a given level and the strength and the duty enforced on it.

30

The relationship between life, duty, and strength

Before studying the types of statistical distributions that can be used to describe failure distributions, we will examine the forms of the duty and strength distributions and of the duty/time-to-failure relationship, so that the manner in which failure distributions derive from them can be appreciated. We will make this examination by using laboratory results of fatigue tests which represent the general case. It must be appreciated that the distributions of failures of parts can differ appreciably from those of laboratory specimens; we will study this at a later stage.

Relationship between life and duty where the initial strength remains constant This relationship can be expressed in the form

$$\frac{1}{D} = b \log_e t + K, \tag{4.1}$$

where D is the duty
t is the time to failure
b and K are constants.

So that if we plot the reciprocal of the stress or load (duty) against the log of the time to failure, a straight line should result. An example is shown in Fig. 4.4 which shows fatigue-test data for an aluminium alloy in both the heat-treated and annealed condition. We may wish to estimate the change in time to failure that will occur if we change the duty, or alternatively, if we have failures, we wish to estimate how much the stress, or other

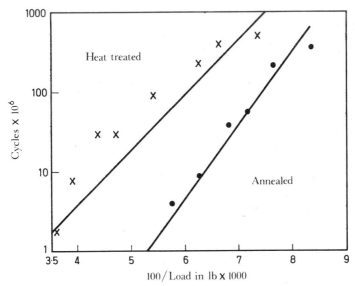

Fig. 4.4 Life of aluminium

31

degrading parameter, must be reduced in order to extend the life a given amount.

From eq. (4.1), and considering two levels of duty,

$$\frac{1}{D_1} = b_1 \log_e t_1 + K_1,$$

$$\frac{1}{D_2} = b_2 \log_e t_2 + K_2.$$

Subtracting (assuming $b_1 = b_2 = b$), we obtain

$$\frac{1}{D_1} - \frac{1}{D_2} = b \log \frac{t_1}{t_2} + K_1 - K_2.$$

The values of K_1 and K_2 can be assumed approximately equal, since this constant relates to the type of degrading mechanism.

It can be shown that $1/x$ is an approximation to $1 - 0.78 \log x$ for values of x between 1 and 2. Some resulting values for comparison are then

$1/x$	1	0·833	0·715	0·625	0·556	0·500
$1 - 0.78 \log x$	1	0·858	0·738	0·633	0·541	0·460

Hence,

$$(1 - a \log D_1) - (1 - a \log D_2) = b \log \frac{t_1}{t_2}$$

$$a \log \frac{D_2}{D_1} = b \log \frac{t_1}{t_2}$$

$$\left(\frac{D_2}{D_1}\right)^B = \frac{t_1}{t_2}, \tag{4.2}$$

where B is a constant dependent on the form of the duty/time-to-failure curve.

The truth of this equation has been demonstrated on innumerable occasions and values of B established, for example for ball-bearing fatigue failures B is approximately 4. For fatigue of steels, B has been found usually to lie between 3 and 10.

Relationship between life and initial strength, where the duty remains constant It appears sensible to relate the rate of change of strength of a material to the rate of change occasioned by the absorption of energy and the loss of strength that has already occurred. We can then write

$$\frac{dM}{dt} = -\lambda(M_0 - M_t)$$

where M is the strength, the subscripts 0 and t relate to original strength and strength at time t, and λ is the rate of change of strength with time.

We will assume λ to be constant and demonstrate that this can be true. Should λ be a function of $M_0 - M_t$ or t the argument used remains valid. We have

$$\frac{\mathrm{d}M}{M_0 - M_t} = -\lambda\,\mathrm{d}t$$

$$\log_e (M_0 - M_t) + c = -\lambda t. \tag{4.3}$$

In the next chapter, we shall study the theoretical form of the strength and failure distributions, and examples which show that many laboratory test results conform very closely to the ideal or general case that we have been considering. These examples also provide substantiation for this equation. In the meantime we will demonstrate its truth in one instance by an example.

The number of examples that are available for study is limited, because of the difficulties in trying to measure initial strength parameters and then relating them to the times to failure under a given duty. The initial strength parameters must be the only ones that significantly affect the lifetime, and the method of measurement must be non-destructive, as otherwise variability tends to obscure the relationship.

Our example relates to low-cycle fatigue of a creep-resistant stainless steel and has been taken from the work of Howard Brook and Graham Ellison. They explored the yield strength of the surface layers of fatigue test pieces by passing a.c. current along them and noting the tensile load on the test piece that was required to cause a change in the characteristic of the resistance or inductance of the test piece. The stress at which this change in the characteristic occurs has been termed the *true elastic limit*. Since the a.c. current concentrates at the surface the results relate to the condition at the surface.

A plot of the true elastic limit against time *before* failure is shown in Fig. 4.5 for alternating loads of 44 and 48 tons/in.² (68 and 74 hbar). It may be noted that all the specimens tested at a particular stress conformed to the same line within a reasonable margin of experimental error. Another point to note is that the true elastic limit at failure was the same for both stresses.

With values for M_0 of 44 tons/in.², the data given in Fig. 4.5 has been transformed and is shown replotted as $\log_e (M_0 - M_N)$ against N in Fig. 4.6, M_N being the true elastic limit after N cycles. The resulting straight line provides some measure of substantiation for eq. (4.3).

The lines in Fig. 4.6 can be used to estimate the cycles to produce values of M_N for given values of M_0 between 44 tons/in.² and the strength at failure, 29 tons/in.² (45 hbar). Figure 4.7 is an extension of Fig. 4.6 that has been produced in this way. A series of lines have been drawn for the 44 tons/in.^{2} stress condition representing different values of M_0. The vertical scale has been annotated in terms of M_N, the values of M_N at zero cycles being M_0.

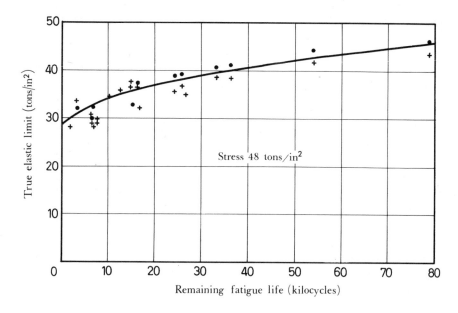

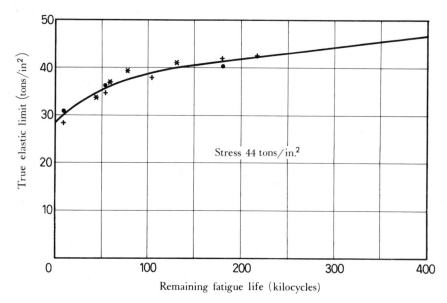

Fig. 4.5   Corrosion resistant stainless steel

The values of initial strength will be definable by a probability distribution and in Fig. 4.6 such a distribution has been shown. The resulting distribution of cycles to failure is also included. It is apparent that these two distributions will follow the same form except that while the initial strength distribution is on a log base scale, that for cycles to failure is on a linear scale.

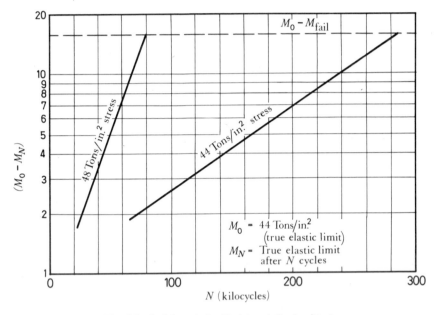

Fig. 4.6 Stainless steel subject to rotating bend tests

Our studies so far have oversimplified the true situation, in as much as there may be two rates of deterioration before failure occurs. For example, the deterioration that produces a crack and the propagation of the crack to failure, as in the case of fatigue failures, will proceed at different rates. Where final fracture occurs from a crack the depth of crack before fracture is also a variable dependent on the fracture toughness of the material. We have the situation where the time to failure is dependent on the variabilities of

(a) The initial strength with regard to crack formation
(b) The strength, at time of crack formation with regard to crack propagation
(c) The size of crack required to cause fracture.

The initial strength we have referred to previously embodied all these variables. If we wish to show the variables separately the diagram given in Fig. 4.7 must be supplemented by a diagram of the form shown in Fig. 4.8.

35

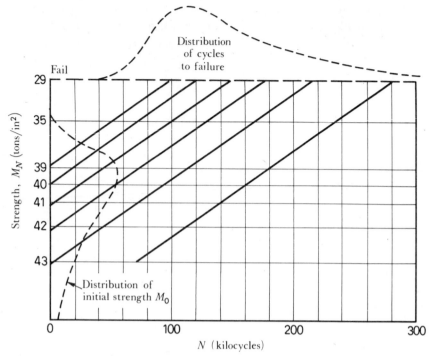

Fig. 4.7   Relationship between initial strength and failure distributions derived from Figs. 4.5 and 4.6

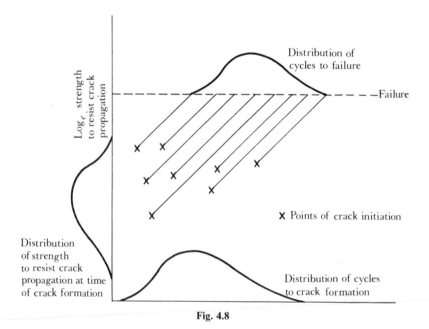

Fig. 4.8

This figure has been drawn assuming that no relationship exists between cycles to crack formation and crack propagation. In practice there may be some relationship, for example, the harder the material the more resistant it will be to crack formation but the propagation rate will be more rapid, giving an inverse relationship.

The figure also assumes that the rate of crack propagation can be represented by a straight line, in the same way as the rate of deterioration found by Brook and Ellison and shown in Fig. 4.6. This latter assumption can be true in the ideal case, as can be shown by reference to studies carried out on the rate of crack development with time by Frost and Dugdale, who produced short cracks mechanically in the middle of sheet specimens, and observed the rate of growth during subsequent fatigue bend tests. They established the relationship

$$\log_e \text{ crack length} = aN + b,$$

and confirmed that this was true for a variety of materials. It will be seen that this equation conforms to the general equation (4.3) if the crack length is regarded as proportional to strength. A typical result from Dugdale's work is shown in Fig. 4.9, and the similarity between it and Fig. 4.6 is apparent.

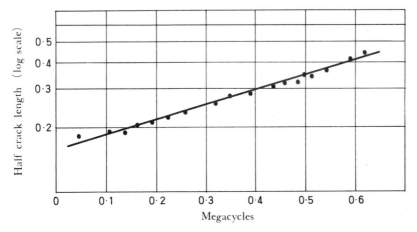

Fig. 4.9   Crack propagation in mild steel sheet

The case where the duty causing final failure differs from that causing degradation   We will now consider the case, referred to earlier in this chapter, where a part is weakened by some mechanism not associated with its loading, and fails due to the imposition of the load.

The appropriate diagram is shown in Fig. 4.10, which is similar to Fig. 4.3 but re-drawn to illustrate the distributions of strength at given times.

The distribution of the load that causes failure is shown on the right-hand side of the diagram, a histogram being used to indicate that it is different from the normal duty and that it consists of isolated occurrences of high load applications. The histogram defines the magnitude and frequency of the load applications. If these are defined we can clearly derive a failure distribution.

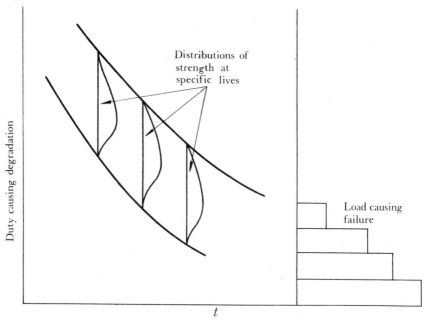

Fig. 4.10

Failure rate and safety factor

It is now time to consider why there can still be a positive failure rate even though a reasonable safety factor is being employed. If the variability of the material strength is small, then the concept of a safety factor is valid

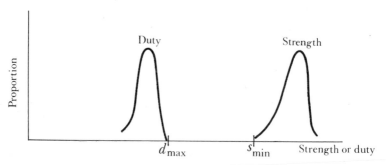

Fig. 4.11

38

(Fig. 4.11). In this case,

$$\text{Safety factor} = \frac{\text{Minimum strength}}{\text{Maximum duty}} = \frac{s_{min}}{d_{max}}.$$

For a safety factor well above 1·0, the failure rate is zero, and the reliability unit (= 100 per cent).

Where the variability of the duty loading and/or the variability of the strength is large, then safety factors become meaningless when expressed in a simple form (Fig. 4.12). The failure rate is positive even though the safety factor, expressed as

$$\text{Safety factor} = \frac{\text{Average strength}}{\text{Average duty}} = \frac{s_{av}}{d_{av}},$$

may be well above 1·0.

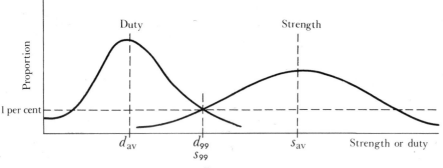

Fig. 4.12

The safety factor based on 99 per cent probabilities may well be about 1·0 for the case shown in Fig. 4.12. That is,

$$\frac{\text{Minimum strength for 99 per cent of material}}{\text{Maximum duty for 99 per cent of occurrences}} = \frac{s_{99}}{d_{99}} \approx 1\cdot0.$$

Under these circumstances we can expect failures on $\frac{1}{100} \times \frac{1}{100} = \frac{1}{10000}$ of the applications of the load. If the load is applied once per day, then this gives a failure rate of $\frac{365}{10000} \approx \frac{1}{30}$ per year, or an average of 1 failure per year for a population of 30. The average safety factor may be 3 or 4 for this case.

Safety factors in practice may be based on the idea of 'minimum properties' where minimum is defined in a manner appropriate to the industry, and could be based on 99 per cent properties, 99·9 per cent properties, or 99·99 per cent properties. A large amount of data is necessary to define the 99·9 per cent or 99·99 per cent properties precisely, and with good quality control and adequate non-destructive testing, 99 per cent properties are nearly always adequate for practical purposes.

39

5

The case of increasing failure rate with time when the duty is constant: the normal and log normal distributions

We have explored ways in which the failure distribution can be related to strength and duty distributions, but before we can examine the various forms of failure distribution that we are likely to encounter in practice, we must study the probable forms of the initial strength and duty distributions from which the failure distribution is derived. In this chapter we shall start this process by looking at a distribution that is the commonest form of the initial strength distribution and examining the failure distribution that derives from it under constant duty conditions.

We will approach the problem of the form of the initial strength distribution by again considering cases of fatigue failures. Since fatigue is a surface effect, the initial strength is that at the surface of the material. Taking a very small area of the surface we can list some of the factors that affect the fatigue strength as follows:

(a) The condition of the surface (finish, etc.)
(b) The amount of impurity in the material at the surface
(c) The amount of work to which the material at the surface has been subjected
(d) The surface hardness
(e) The grain structure
(f) The molecular structure.

There are clearly other factors that affect the fatigue strength as well as those listed. The important point is that the initial strength is derived from a large number of different factors.

Now each of these factors has a distribution. We do not know the forms of these distributions, and for the purposes of our argument we will assume that they are of irregular non-symmetrical forms.

At this stage we will introduce the best known of all statistical distributions, the *normal distribution*. This is a symmetrical distribution that is described by mathematical functions which can be deduced when the principles of pure chance are applied to a population of infinite size. It occurs frequently in nature: for example, the distribution of men's heights is found to be a normal one. The general form can be seen in Fig. 5.1.

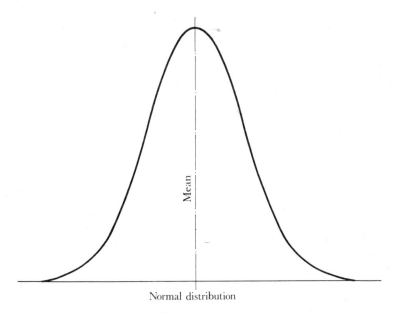

Normal distribution

Fig. 5.1   The normal distribution: general form

We will also introduce one of the most important theorems in statistics called the *central limit theorem*, which states that *the sum of N independent distributions of any form is approximately normally distributed when N is large.*

This can be put another way. *The distribution of the mean of samples of equal size taken at random from independent distributions approaches the normal distribution as the sample size increases, regardless of the form of the independent distribution.*

Applying the central limit theorem to our example of fatigue failures we see that whatever the distributions of the factors that affect the initial strength, the distribution of this strength can be expected to be normal provided that enough factors are involved. Consideration of the factors listed will show that each case is dependent on a number of other factors so that their distributions may well be approaching normal distributions.

The reader may feel that he would like some substantiation of these statements, and while the proofs can be found in some books on statistics, the following simple practical exercise with a pack of cards will provide some verification. If we take cards of a particular suit we have a square distribution, where there is an equal probability of selecting any particular card.

ACE	2	3	4	5	6	7	8	9	10

For the exercise a number of sets of cards, each of one suit, say from ace to 5, are used. Taking say three such sets to start with, cards are selected at random and the total number of pips added together. This is repeated a number of times—at least fifty for preference—and the results plotted in the form of a histogram. It will be found that the square distributions combined in this way have produced a distribution that has a hump in the middle. The exercise is then repeated with a larger number of sets of cards and it will be found that the hump increases, showing that the greater the number of distributions the greater the tendency for the sums of the samples to centralize. If desired, the square distributions can be altered somewhat by adding duplicate cards at one end or the other. The effect of this will be seen in the histogram but again it will be found that the larger the number of card sets used the less the effect of odd biased suit sets will be.

If the reader is enthusiastic enough to carry out this exercise he will find that in addition to the fact that the tendency to produce a symmetrical hump increases rapidly with the number of samples, the histograms he produces will be of a very irregular form, since results cannot be expected to work out in accordance with the actual probabilities in the short term. It is necessary to take very large numbers of samples indeed for the chances of getting a particular value to be able to exert sufficient influence to provide him with an even histogram that conforms to the theory. The point is made that when a few sample components are checked for their initial strength, the results may appear not to conform very closely to a normal distribution even though this would result if a large number of components were tested.

It is worth a comment that the normal distribution is used extensively in statistical quality control where the dimensions produced by machine tools are found to conform to it, because a large number of small influences determine the dimension that is produced.

Defining the normal distribution

We will now examine the normal distribution in more detail. Before we can use it to describe distributions that actually occur, we must be able to define it mathematically, that is, have an expression that describes its probability distribution function.

Referring to Fig. 5.1, the distribution is located at some point on the base scale, and defining this point fixes the position of the distribution. Since it is a symmetrical distribution, it is natural to fix it by defining the

42

average or mean value. We will give it the notation $\bar{x}$, signifying the average of the recorded values x_1, x_2, x_3, etc. Having fixed the position, the only other parameter necessary to define a normal distribution is a measure of its dispersion, and the measure used is called the *standard deviation*. This relates to the amount of dispersion on either side of the mean, and is denoted by σ.

The standard deviation is the root mean square of all values of the deviations of the population from the mean, or mathematically,

$$\sigma = \sqrt{\frac{(x_1 - \bar{x})^2 + (x_2 - \bar{x})^2 + \ldots + (x_N - \bar{x})^2}{N}},$$

where $(x_1 - \bar{x})$, $(x_2 - \bar{x})$, etc., are the deviations from the mean, and N is the number in the population.

It will be seen that it is necessary to use the squares of the deviates so that all the terms are positive, and this leads naturally to the use of the root mean square. In practice, the calculation of σ can only result in a best estimate and it is shown in books on statistics that it is preferable to use $N - 1$ as the denominator in place of N, though as the size of the data increases this correction becomes negligible.

We are now in a position to define the probability distribution function, and calling this $f(x)$, we have

$$f(x) = \frac{1}{\sigma\sqrt{2\pi}} \exp\left[-\frac{1}{2}\left(\frac{x - \bar{x}}{\sigma}\right)^2 \right], \tag{5.1}$$

$x - \bar{x}$ being the deviation from the mean. Then the cumulative probability distribution $F(x)$ is

$$F(x) = \frac{1}{\sigma\sqrt{2\pi}} \int_{-\infty}^{x} \exp\left[-\frac{1}{2}\left(\frac{x - \bar{x}}{\sigma}\right)^2 \right] dx. \tag{5.2}$$

This expression is difficult to handle but it can be simplified by a process known as standardizing the normal curve, which simply involves substituting u for $(x - \bar{x})/\sigma$.

This substitution is equivalent to putting $\bar{x} = 0$ and $\sigma = 1$, in which case $u = x$. With this substitution, values of $F(u)$ have been worked out for different values of u; these are tabulated in standard works on statistics. Now,

$$u = \frac{x - \bar{x}}{\sigma} \quad \text{when } \bar{x} = 0,$$

so that if we convert x into the equivalent number of standard deviations, we can use the table to obtain $F(x)$ for given values of x. Reference to Fig. 5.2 will make this clear: in this figure a normal distribution has been divided

43

into increments corresponding to deviations of 1, 2, and 3 standard deviations from the mean.

We will consider the line marked A in the figure which is shown as one standard deviation from the mean. One standard deviation occurs at $u = 1$. From the standard tables, for $u = 1$, $F(u) = 0.8413$, which means that the area to the left of line A is equal to 84·13 per cent of the whole. The percentages of the increments defined by 1, 2, and 3 standard deviations are shown in Fig. 5.2.

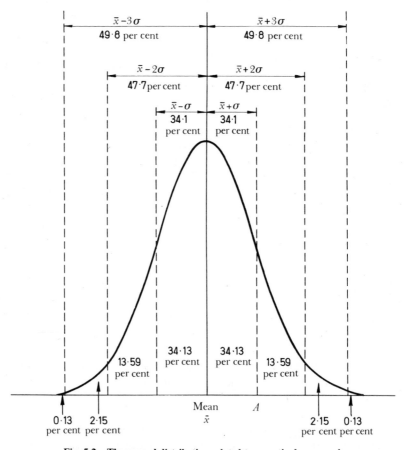

Fig. 5.2   The normal distribution related to a particular example

Calculating the mean and standard deviation

An example will illustrate the calculation of the mean and standard deviation. The example relates to the production of a dimension, actually a milling operation with a nominal dimension of 1·00. The data and the

44

calculation are set out in Table 5.1. It will be noted that the mean has been calculated by averaging the deviations from a suitably selected value in order to simplify the arithmetic.

Table 5.1

	Calculation of mean			Calculation of standard deviation		
Dimen-sion	Fre-quency of occur-rence	Deviation from selected value of 1·010	Deviation × frequency	Deviation from mean	Square of deviation from mean	Square of deviation × frequency
x	f	$1·010 - x$	$f(1·010 - x)$	$x - \bar{x}$	$(x - \bar{x})^2$	$f(x - \bar{x})^2$
0·989	1	0·021	0·021	$-0·87 \times 10^{-2}$	$0·757 \times 10^{-4}$	$0·757 \times 10^{-4}$
0·990	2	0·020	0·040	$-0·77 \times 10^{-2}$	$0·593 \times 10^{-4}$	$1·186 \times 10^{-4}$
0·991	1	0·019	0·019	$-0·67 \times 10^{-2}$	$0·449 \times 10^{-4}$	$0·449 \times 10^{-4}$
0·992	4	0·018	0·072	$-0·57 \times 10^{-2}$	$0·325 \times 10^{-4}$	$1·300 \times 10^{-4}$
0·993	3	0·017	0·051	$-0·47 \times 10^{-2}$	$0·221 \times 10^{-4}$	$0·663 \times 10^{-4}$
0·994	2	0·016	0·032	$-0·37 \times 10^{-2}$	$0·137 \times 10^{-4}$	$0·274 \times 10^{-4}$
0·995	4	0·015	0·060	$-0·27 \times 10^{-2}$	$0·073 \times 10^{-4}$	$0·292 \times 10^{-4}$
0·996	7	0·014	0·098	$-0·17 \times 10^{-2}$	$0·029 \times 10^{-4}$	$0·203 \times 10^{-4}$
0·997	6	0·013	0·078	$-0·07 \times 10^{-2}$	$0·005 \times 10^{-4}$	$0·030 \times 10^{-4}$
0·998	8	0·012	0·096	$+0·03 \times 10^{-2}$	$0·001 \times 10^{-4}$	$0·008 \times 10^{-4}$
0·999	5	0·011	0·055	$+0·13 \times 10^{-2}$	$0·017 \times 10^{-4}$	$0·085 \times 10^{-4}$
1·000	4	0·010	0·040	$+0·23 \times 10^{-2}$	$0·053 \times 10^{-4}$	$0·212 \times 10^{-4}$
1·001	3	0·009	0·027	$+0·33 \times 10^{-2}$	$0·109 \times 10^{-4}$	$0·327 \times 10^{-4}$
1·002	2	0·008	0·016	$+0·43 \times 10^{-2}$	$0·185 \times 10^{-4}$	$0·370 \times 10^{-4}$
1·003	5	0·007	0·035	$+0·53 \times 10^{-2}$	$0·281 \times 10^{-4}$	$1·405 \times 10^{-4}$
1·004	3	0·006	0·018	$+0·63 \times 10^{-2}$	$0·397 \times 10^{-4}$	$1·191 \times 10^{-4}$
1·005	2	0·005	0·010	$+0·73 \times 10^{-2}$	$0·533 \times 10^{-4}$	$1·066 \times 10^{-4}$
1·006	1	0·004	0·004	$+0·83 \times 10^{-2}$	$0·689 \times 10^{-4}$	$0·689 \times 10^{-4}$
Total	63		0·772		$4·854 \times 10^{-4}$	$10·507 \times 10^{-4}$

$$\text{Mean} = 1·010 - \frac{0·772}{63} = 0·9977 \qquad \text{Standard deviation} = \sqrt{\frac{10·507 \times 10^{-4}}{63 - 1}} = 0·00412$$

Having worked out the mean and standard deviation we can express values of x in terms of u and by using the tables we can plot the probability distribution function. This is shown in Fig. 5.2, together with a histogram (Fig. 5.3) of the actual dimensions produced. It will be noted that the histogram is rather irregular, but this is what normally happens where we are considering a sample or any quantity of results that is not a large number. As the number of results increases, the chances of getting the appropriate number relative to each value increase, and the results presented in histogram form become more regular.

Approximate estimation of the standard deviation

A rough estimate of σ can be made where the sample size is small, less than 15 from the *range* of the sample, that, is the difference between the

45

highest and lowest values. Then,

$$\sigma \text{ estimated } = R/\sqrt{n}, \tag{5.3}$$

where R is the range,

        n is the sample size.

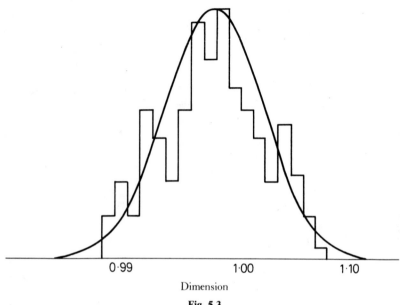

Dimension

Fig. 5.3

The extremes of the normal distribution

It will be noted that the integration in eq. (5.2) was from minus infinity. The term

$$\frac{1}{\sigma\sqrt{2\pi}} \int_{-\infty}^{+\infty} \exp\left[-\frac{1}{2}\frac{(x-\bar{x})^2}{2\sigma}\right] \tag{5.4}$$

is equal to one, so that for a probability of one we must consider the area under the curve between plus and minus infinity.

The normal distribution accordingly provides us with a probability, though a remote one, where the deviation $(x - \bar{x})$ from the mean value $(\bar{x})$ is infinitely great in both plus and minus directions. Taking the case of the initial strength of a component, it is clearly impossible to obtain components that approach infinite strength or infinite weakness; there are limits to the strength which apply when the component conforms to its specification. The same considerations apply in the case of other engineering variables: for example, the dimension that is produced by a machine tool or the output of a series of pumps. While it is a sound argument that

46

the initial strength or any other engineering property that is derived from many variable factors conforms to the normal distribution over most of its variable range, the tail ends of the actual distribution will not stretch out in the same way as the theoretical one, and we may never get a case where the probability of 1 in 1000 or even 1 in 100 is exceeded. Thus, it is unwise to use the distribution when considering more remote probabilities.

Plotting the normal distribution

Given a set of data regarding some engineering parameter that considerations tell us will probably conform to the normal distribution, a sound way to proceed is to plot the cumulative distribution function in the same way as we have plotted mortality curves. This will give us some indication as to whether our supposition was correct, and will provide a simpler way of estimating the standard deviation than that given previously. It may be that the distribution we are investigating is normal over most of the curve, but for some reason departs from normality at the lower end.

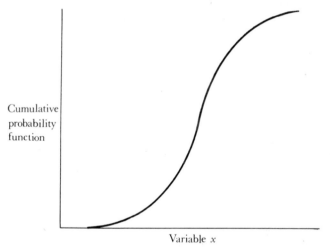

Fig. 5.4   Linear representation of the normal distribution cumulative probability function

This can clearly be important if we are considering strength or some other parameter that can affect failures. Plotting the cumulative distribution function should indicate whether this is the case.

A normal distribution produces a cumulative distribution function of the general form shown in Fig. 5.4 when plotted on linear graph paper. Special paper is available where the probability scale has been adjusted so as to change the S-shaped curve shown in this figure to a straight line. This is known as normal probability paper and is illustrated in Fig. 5.5.

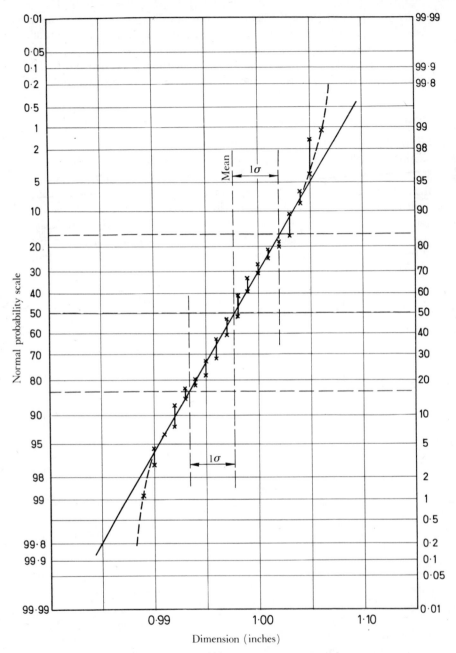

Fig. 5.5 Example of use of normal probability paper

The points are calculated by one of the methods given for mortality curves. Assuming that a straight line fits the points reasonably well it will provide us with an estimate of the distribution when this is normal. If the use of probability paper has failed to eliminate the S-shape of Fig. 5.4, then the distribution is not normal but skewed. We shall look at ways of dealing with such cases shortly.

As an example of the use of normal probability paper the data used in the previous example has been plotted in Fig. 5.5. Table 5.2 shows this data with the appropriate median rank value. Note that the tails of the distribution depart from normality due to manufacturing constrictions.

Table 5.2

Dimension	Frequency of occurrence	Rank number	Median rank
0·989	1	1	0·011
0·990	2	2–3	0·027–0·043
0·991	1	4	0·058
0·992	4	5–8	0·074–0·121
0·993	3	9–11	0·137–0·169
0·994	2	12–13	0·185–0·200
0·995	4	14–17	0·216–0·263
0·996	7	18–24	0·279–0·374
0·997	6	25–30	0·390–0·468
0·998	8	31–38	0·484–0·595
0·999	5	39–43	0·610–0·674
1·000	4	44–47	0·689–0·737
1·001	3	48–50	0·752–0·784
1·002	2	51–52	0·800–0·815
1·003	5	53–57	0·831–0·894
1·004	3	58–60	0·910–0·942
1·005	2	61–62	0·957–0·973
1·006	1	63	0·989

The mean can be read off at the 50 per cent probability point and σ can be obtained by taking the difference between the 16 per cent and 84 per cent probability point and the mean, since the deviate of $x - \bar{x} = \sigma$ represented a probability of 34 per cent either side of the mean. Examination will show that these are in agreement with the calculated values.

If our argument that the initial strength distribution can be expected to be normal is correct, then it is to be expected that other measurable strength parameters will be normally distributed. This is frequently found to be true, but cases are also met in which a dominant factor that is not normally distributed, for example some form of imperfection, distorts the form of the distribution. As an example, the distributions arising from a large number of tensile tests on three types of high-strength carbon steel are given in Fig. 5.6, plotted on normal probability paper. Two of these distributions are seen to be normally distributed with departures at the

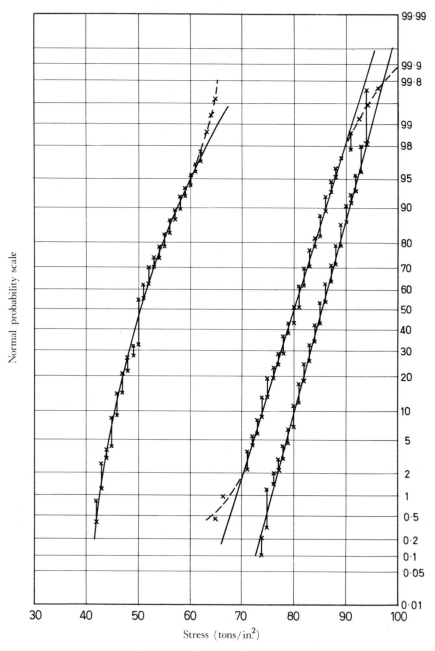

Fig. 5.6   Tensile tests on three types of carbon steel

tails. These departures provide further evidence of the dangers of assuming that a normal distribution will define the actual state of affairs in the remote probability regions. The third distribution is definitely not normal. We have a case where it has been distorted.

We have seen that a failure distribution can be dependent on a number of strength distributions: for example, those of initial strength with regard to both crack formation and crack propagation, and fracture toughness. Now even if these distributions in themselves are not normal, as they can be expected to be, the application of the central limit theorem tends to produce a combined distribution that is sensibly normal. We can treat the initial strength distribution as a single distribution, even though there are various stages of deterioration prior to final failure. We can also expect this combined initial strength distribution to be normal in the general case.

Referring to Fig. 5.6, we can regard the skewed distribution of initial strength as being a normal distribution that has been distorted by plotting on a log base, in which case the time-to-failure distribution can also be described in this way. Such a distribution is called a *log normal distribution* and we can expect it to describe the failure distribution in the general case.

The log normal distribution

We can perform exactly the same calculations for a log normal distribution as we did for a normal distribution, only it is necessary to convert the base scale to log values before we perform the calculation, and then convert them back again after it is completed.

The probability density function is

$$f(t) = \frac{1}{\sigma t \sqrt{2\pi}} \exp\left\{ -\frac{1}{2}\left(\frac{\log_e (t - t_x)}{\sigma} \right)^2 \right\}. \tag{5.5}$$

The cumulative distribution function is given by

$$F(t) = \int_0^t f(t)\, dt = \frac{1}{\sigma \sqrt{2\pi}} \int_0^t \frac{1}{t} \exp\left\{ -\frac{1}{2}\left(\frac{\log_e (t - t_x)}{\sigma} \right)^2 \right\} dt, \tag{5.6}$$

and the local failure rate by

$$Z(t) = \frac{f(t)}{1 - F(t)} = \frac{\dfrac{1}{t} \exp\left\{ -\dfrac{1}{2}\left(\dfrac{\log_e (t - t_x)}{\sigma} \right)^2 \right\}}{\displaystyle\int_t^\infty \frac{1}{t} \exp\left\{ -\frac{1}{2}\left(\frac{\log_e (t - t_x)}{\sigma} \right)^2 \right\}}.$$

Life has again been made easier for us by the production of log normal probability paper which is similar to normal probability paper in as much as the probability scale conforms to the normal distribution, the

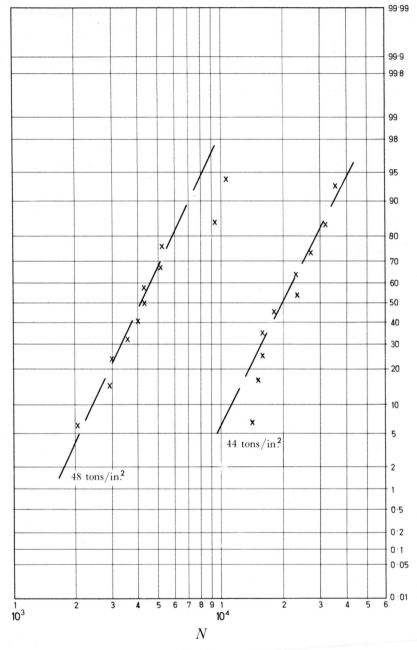

Fig. 5.7

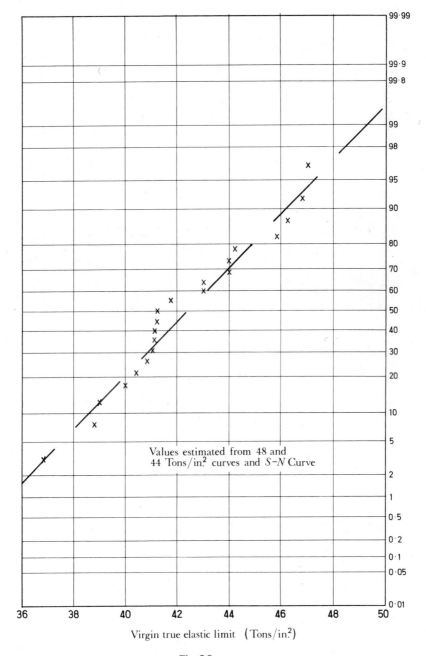

Fig. 5.8

linear scale being replaced by a log scale. A specimen sheet is given in Fig. 5.7.

Examples of failure distributions that are log normally distributed

The truth of the relationship between initial strength and life given by eq. (4.3) can now be further demonstrated by examples.

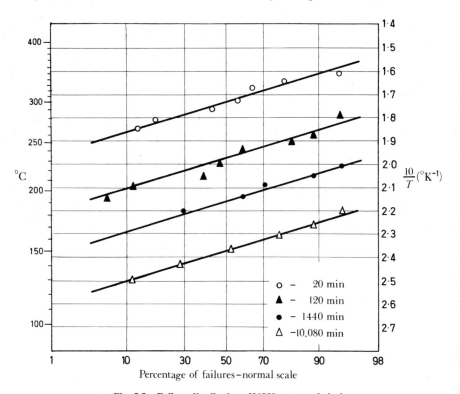

Fig. 5.9   Failure distribution: 2N559, vacuum baked

We will take two examples where both the initial strength and failure distributions are known. The first of these is taken from Brook and Ellison's previously mentioned fatigue work on creep-resistant stainless steels. The results of fatigue tests on a number of specimens carried out at a constant 44 and 48 tons/in.² (68 and 74 hbar) are shown in Fig. 5.7 on log normal probability paper; general conformity with the log normal distribution will be observed.

The cycles to failure given by the points in this figure have been used to estimate the initial true elastic limit of the specimens by means of the curves given in Fig. 4.5. In this way, a distribution of initial true elastic limit has been deduced, and is shown on normal probability paper in Fig. 5.8—again there is general conformity.

The second example is taken from work done at the Bell Telephone laboratories and concerns work on 2N559 germanium transistors. The duty that caused failure was exposure to temperature. The transistors were heated in a furnace for a period, removed and tested for failure. If they survived they were returned to the furnace and exposed to a higher temperature, the process being repeated until all had failed. The results of these tests are shown plotted in Fig. 5.9. The vertical scale is the inverse of the absolute temperature and the horizontal a normal probability scale. The failure points have been corrected for degradation due to exposure at temperatures lower than that which caused failure.

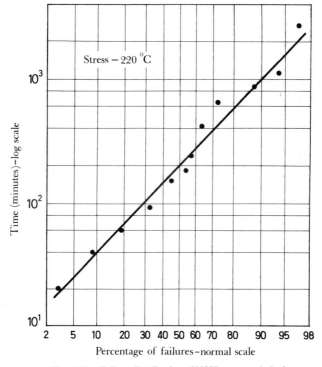

Fig. 5.10   Failure distribution: 2N559, vacuum baked

The lines shown on the graph relate to exposure times of 20 minutes, 120 minutes, 1440 minutes (1 day) and 10^4 minutes (1 week) and show the distributions of initial strength, as defined by the inverse of the duty. It will be seen that this initial strength is normally distributed.

Further tests were done on the transistors by exposing them to a temperature of 220°C, which was expected to result in 50 per cent failures in

55

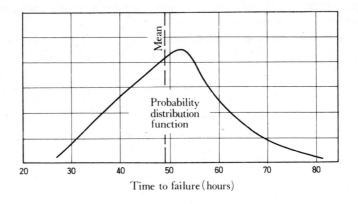

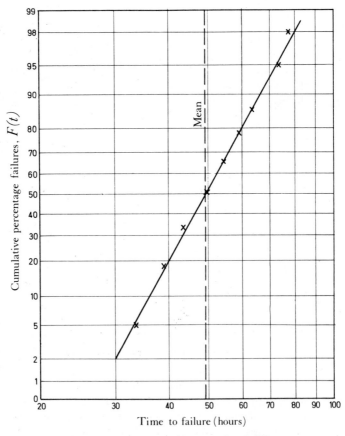

**Fig. 5.11 Example of use of log normal probability paper:
distribution of creep-test results from sample turbine-blade material**

a few hours. In this case, the temperature was held constant and the transistors removed from the furnace at intervals and tested. The resulting mortality curve is shown in Fig. 5.10 on log normal probability paper, and it can be seen that it is a good approximation to the log normal distribution.

Some further examples in which failure distributions are log normal, the initial strength distribution being unknown, add weight to the previous arguments. The first of these examples covers the routine testing of samples of turbine blade material for resistance to creep at high temperature. To reduce the test time, these tests were carried out at higher temperatures and stress than the material would normally encounter. For analysis, the results were broken down into lifetime bands, and the points on the curve given in Fig. 5.11 represent the cumulative percentage failed at lifetime-band increments. It will be seen that the failure distribution is a good approximation to the log normal.

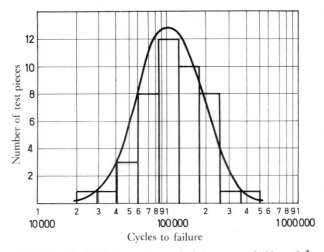

Fig. 5.12 Tension fatigue tests: nominal stress range 0–46 tons/in^2.

Two further examples relate to work done in industry and have been taken from a paper by Frank Nixon. They are illustrated in Figs. 5.12 and 5.13 and show the general form of the distributions of particular fatigue tests plotted as probability distribution functions on a log base scale. In both cases they approximate to log normal distributions.

Departures from the log normal distribution

All the examples given in this chapter relate to tests where only a small section or area of material was subject to test. Such tests often produce a log normal distribution, but we shall see later that where the section or area of material subject to test is increased, the form of the distribution is affected.

Should the factors that lead to the variation in the initial strength contain a particularly dominant one whose distribution is skewed, this will clearly distort the normal form of the strength distribution and like-wise the log normal form of the failure distribution. We can accordingly only regard the log normal distribution as representing the general case. In the next chapters we will examine the Weibull and extreme value distri-butions that cover cases where such distortion occurs.

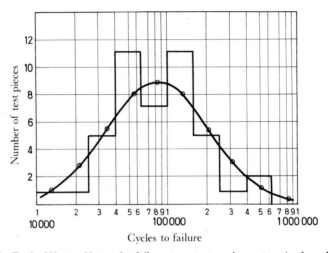

Fig. 5.13   Fortiweld butt welds tested to failure at constant maximum stress (cycles on log scale)

6

The Weibull, binomial, and Poisson distributions: confidence levels

Of all the statistical distributions that are available to help reliability engineers to analyse particular situations, the Weibull distribution can be regarded as the most valuable; to introduce this distribution, we will digress from the line of argument that we have been pursuing, in order that we can utilize it in our subsequent studies.

We have argued that the initial strength should be normally distributed, but since this is dependent on it deriving from a large number of variables that affect it to a relatively similar degree, we must regard the normal distribution as a special case although it occurs with great regularity. We require a distribution that will describe the life to failure when the initial strength distribution is not normal.

Such a distribution is the Weibull distribution, which was devised by Professor Weibull for describing the results of fatigue tests, and which embraces a great variety of forms including one that closely approximates to the normal. Weibull called his original paper on the subject 'A Distribution of Wide Applicability', and we shall see how apt this is.

We approach the Weibull distribution by considering eq. (1.8):

$$R(t) = \exp\left[-\int_0^t Z(t) \, dt \right].$$

If we can establish an expression for $Z(t)$ that describes a wide range of probable failure rates, we shall have a cumulative distribution function that gives us $R(t)$ for a range of failure distributions. The simplest form of expression is

$$Z(t) = at^b,$$

which gives us

$$R(t) = \exp\left(-\frac{at^{b+1}}{b+1} \right) = \exp\left[-\left(\frac{t}{A}\right)^{b+1} \right],$$

59

where

$$A = \left(\frac{b + 1}{a}\right)^{1/(b+1)}$$

This is similar to the Weibull cumulative distribution function, which is

$$R(t) = \exp\left[-\left(\frac{t - \gamma}{\eta}\right)^{\beta}\right], \qquad (6.1)$$

where t is the time to failure
  γ is the time at which $F(t) = 0$ and is a datum parameter
  η is the characteristic life and is a scale parameter
  β is a shape parameter.

Then

$$F(t) = 1 - \exp\left[-\left(\frac{t - \gamma}{\eta}\right)^{\beta}\right]. \qquad (6.2)$$

From eq. (1.4),

$$f(t) = \frac{dF(t)}{dt} = \frac{\beta(t - \gamma)^{\beta - 1}}{\eta^{\beta}} \exp\left[-\left(\frac{t - \gamma}{\eta}\right)^{\beta}\right]. \qquad (6.3)$$

From eq. (1.5),

$$Z(t) = \frac{f(t)}{R(t)} = \beta \frac{(t - \gamma)^{\beta - 1}}{\eta^{\beta}} \qquad (6.4)$$

It will be seen that the Weibull is a three-parameter distribution (γ, η, and β), whereas the normal and log normal had only two controlling parameters, the mean and the standard deviation.*

The datum parameter γ is the cause of most of the complication associated with the Weibull distribution. We will accordingly adopt a simplified approach and make $\gamma = 0$, which simply means that we are assuming $F(t) = 0$ at $t = 0$ and that there will be a positive value for $F(t)$ at all values of t above zero. With this simplification we will proceed to examine the distribution further.

The Weibull distribution has the great virtue of providing us with a large number of different shapes, some of which are illustrated in Fig. 6.1, which shows the probability density function plotted against t for various values of the shape parameter β, with η maintained constant at 1. Different values of η would have the effect of extending the scale of t without affecting shapes of the distribution. We will examine what happens with various values of β.

* Statistically, the log normal distribution also has three parameters, but for reliability analysis the third parameter can usually be ignored with safety, so we shall treat the log normal as a two-parameter distribution.

1. $\beta < 1$. This is illustrated by curves of $\beta = \frac{1}{3}$ and $\beta = \frac{1}{2}$. Since $Z(t) = \beta t^{\beta-1}/\eta^\beta$, it will be seen that for $\beta < 1$, the power of t becomes negative and accordingly $Z(t)$ decreases as t increases. We have the case of decreasing failure rate with time, the condition that arises when the first part of the bathtub curve is applicable.

2. $\beta = 1$. This is illustrated in Fig. 6.1:

$$Z(t) = \beta t^{\beta-1}/\eta^\beta = 1/\eta.$$

We have a constant local failure rate of $1/\eta$. Also,

$$F(t) = 1 - \exp\left[-\int_0^t \frac{1}{\eta} \, dt \right] = 1 - \exp\left(-\frac{t}{\eta} \right),$$

which describes the negative exponential distribution. Thus, the special case of the Weibull distribution where $\beta = 1$ provides us with the negative exponential distribution, and in this case η is equal to the mean time between failures, m.

3. $1 < \beta < 2$. This is illustrated in Fig. 6.1 by $\beta = 1\frac{2}{3}$ and $\beta = 2$. It will be seen that these cases are skewed distributions, which show a rapid decrease of $f(t)$ as they approach $t = 0$. They clearly represent an increasing failure rate with time.

4. $\beta > 2$. This is illustrated in Fig. 6.1 by $\beta = 2\frac{1}{2}$, etc. At about $\beta = 2$, a change in the form of the distribution occurs and the tail of the distribution as it approaches $t = 0$ tends to become asymptotic with the t-axis in the same manner as the normal distribution. The distribution also becomes more symmetrical as values of β increase. At $\beta = 3 \cdot 2$ the Weibull distribution becomes a good approximation to the normal, though there is some error at the remote probabilities. Higher values of β also produce a distribution which does not depart markedly from the normal.

We will now introduce the datum parameter γ. If we have a failure mode that takes some time to develop, e.g., creep or fatigue, the distribution of failures start at some finite time after a latent period. Where the failure rate is decreasing or is constant, no latent time before failures start is to be expected, and the parameter γ is normally zero where $\beta < 1$. However, a latent period before failures start is likely in all cases where $\beta > 1$, and this will have the effect of pushing the distribution bodily along the t-axis.

Whereas the normal and log normal distributions were datumed on the mean and defined by the mean and deviates from it, the Weibull is datumed from $t = 0$ and defined by values of t. Thus, once the distribution is moved along the t-axis it ceases to conform to the Weibull distribution unless the parameter γ is brought in to restore it to its correct datum, i.e., adjusts the time at which the distribution starts to a value of $t = 0$.

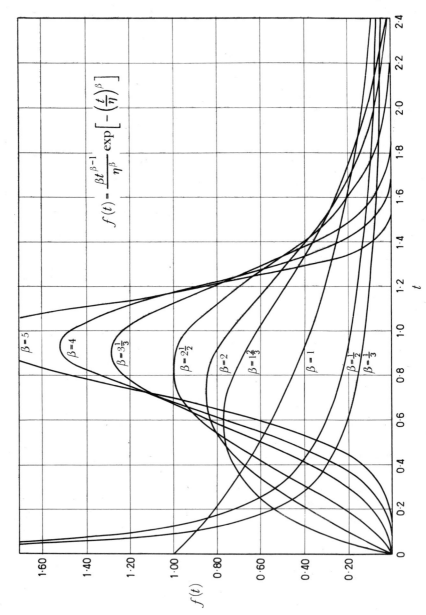

$$f(t) = \frac{\beta t^{\beta-1}}{\eta^{\beta}} \exp\left[-\left(\frac{t}{\eta}\right)^{\beta}\right]$$

Fig. 6.1 The Weibull probability density function for various values of β when $\eta = 1, \gamma = 0$

Plotting the Weibull distribution

In order to be able to use the Weibull distribution in reliability work, we require to plot the mortality curves and, if necessary, to evaluate γ, β, and η for any particular curve. For the purpose of plotting the curves, Weibull probability paper has been made available, and in order that its use may be properly understood, we will develop the equation on which it is based.

We have

$$F(t) = 1 - \exp\left[-\left(\frac{t-\gamma}{\eta}\right)^{\beta}\right]$$

$$\therefore\; 1 - F(t) = \exp\left[-\left(\frac{t-\gamma}{\eta}\right)^{\beta}\right]$$

$$\frac{1}{1-F(t)} = \exp\left(\frac{t-\gamma}{\eta}\right)^{\beta}$$

$$\log_e \frac{1}{1-F(t)} = \left(\frac{t-\gamma}{\eta}\right)^{\beta}$$

$$\log_e \log_e \frac{1}{1-F(t)} = \beta \log_e (t-\gamma) - \beta \log_e \eta. \tag{6.5}$$

For any particular case β and η are constants, so we have produced an equation which results in a straight line if we plot $\log_e \log_e 1/[1 - F(t)]$ against $\log_e (t-\gamma)$, and this is the basis of Weibull probability paper.

Weibull probability paper is illustrated diagrammatically in Fig. 6.2. There are four scales, scale A being $\log_e (t-\gamma)$, scale B $\log_e \log_e 1/[1 - F(t)]$, and scales C and D transformed values, namely, t and $F(t)$.

It will be clear from eq. (6.5) that β gives the slope of the line, and from the diagram it represents the rate of change of failure rate with time. Once a line has been drawn, values of β can easily be found by graphical differentiation, i.e., taking an increment of scale B divided by the equivalent increment of scale A.

If we make

$$\log_e \log_e \frac{1}{1-F(t)} = 0,$$

then from eq. (6.5),

$$\beta \log_e (t-\gamma) = \beta \log_e \eta,$$

and $t - \gamma = \eta$.

Accordingly, η is obtained by reading off the value of t where the line crosses the zero value on scale B, a value that corresponds to $F(t) = 63$ per cent.

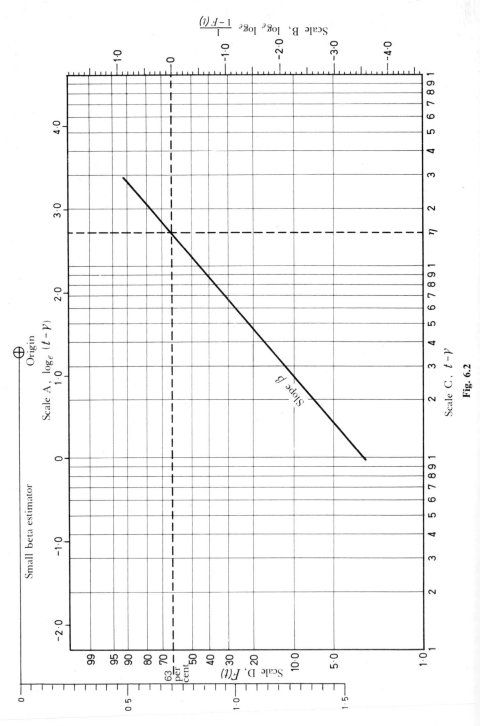

Fig. 6.2

We have seen that the Weibull distribution must have a datum point at $t = 0$. For an actual mortality curve to conform to this requirement there must be a probability of failures at zero time which can occur

(a) when failures are due to purely chance causes
(b) when the form of the distribution is such that the tail becomes asymptotic to the t-axis at low values of t, as occurs in the case of the normal distribution.

In most cases, and particularly where strength distributions are being plotted, the distributions will give a zero probability of failure at some finite value of t. This results in the actual mortality curve taking a concave form on Weibull probability paper. We must subtract γ from values given by this curve in order to make it conform to the Weibull distribution. Methods are given below for estimating γ, and once this estimate has been made, the scale of t is adjusted by subtracting γ so that we are using an actual scale of $t - \gamma$ but annotated with values of t.

Estimation of γ

Method I. The value of γ is guessed and this value subtracted from the values of t corresponding to a number of points on the curve. Fig. 6.3(a) illustrates the principle. The points obtained in this way represent $t - \gamma$ estimated. The process is repeated on a trial-and-error basis until the best estimate of γ is obtained, which results in the points falling on a straight line.

Method II. A method developed by General Motors is illustrated in Fig. 6.3(b). Three lines are drawn parallel to the t-axis equally spaced on the B-scale, the values of t where these lines intersect the curve being t_1, t_2, and t_3. Then,

$$\gamma = t_2 - \frac{(t_3 - t_2)(t_2 - t_1)}{(t_3 - t_2) - (t_2 - t_1)}.$$

The method requires accurate estimation of the values of t_1, t_2, and t_3. It is useful for giving an estimate of γ that can be verified by Method I.

Method III. When we have only a small portion of the curve covering, for example, early failures, neither of the first two methods is applicable. In such cases the portion of the curve that can be plotted frequently departs from a straight line by only a small extent. Where the type of failure is such that it cannot be expected to occur at or near zero, we expect the line to be a curve, even if this is not apparent, and while the line we have drawn adequately describes the distribution over the length that we are able to plot, it is clearly inadvisable to extrapolate it.

65

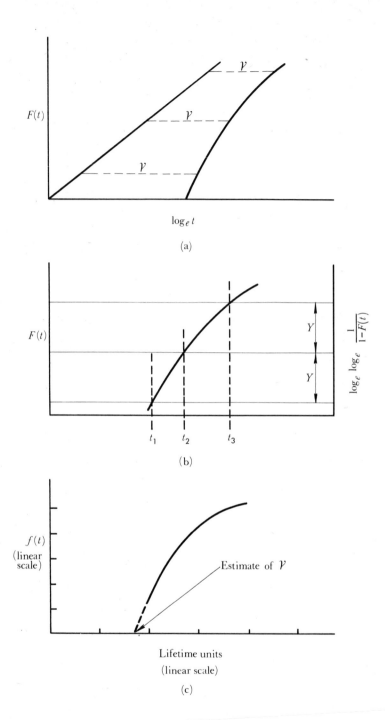

Fig. 6.3

To deal with such cases the author has devised the following approximate method of estimating γ.

The known part of the curve is differentiated and the resulting values of $f(t)$ plotted against t on linear paper. The resultant curve is of one of the forms shown in Fig. 6.1 and, for $1 < \beta < 2$, will approach the vertical at the lower values of $f(t)$. Some intelligent extrapolation down to $f(t) = 0$ will provide an estimation of γ. The method is illustrated in Fig. 6.3(c).

The binomial distribution

For two pieces of equipment A and B whose reliabilities and probabilities of failure are defined as $R(A)$, $R(B)$, and $F(A)$, $F(B)$, we have seen that the probability of both surviving is $R(A)R(B)$, and that of both failing is $F(A)F(B)$.

Now consider the case where one survives and one fails. This can occur in two ways: A failing and B surviving, or B failing and A surviving. The probabilities are

$$F(A)R(B) \quad \text{and} \quad F(B)R(A).$$

Now these two probabilities are independent of one another, and to arrive at the total probability of one failure we add them together. We can now write down all the possible outcomes, the sum of which equals unity:

$$R(A)R(B) + \left[F(A)R(B) + F(B)R(A) \right] + F(A)F(B) = 1.$$

$$\underset{\text{No failures}}{\uparrow} \qquad\qquad \underset{\text{1 failure}}{\uparrow} \qquad\qquad \underset{\text{2 failures}}{\uparrow}$$

If $R(A) = R(B) = R$ (and accordingly $F(A) = F(B) = F$), this becomes

$$R^2 + 2FR + F^2 = 1;$$

that is,

$$(R + F)^2 = 1.$$

Next, consider three pieces of equipment A, B, and C. It is clear that the probability of no failures is $R(A)R(B)R(C)$ and that of three failures is $F(A)F(B)F(C)$.

For the case of one failure, either A, B, or C can fail.

For A failing the probability is $F(A)R(B)R(C)$
For B failing the probability is $F(B)R(A)R(C)$
For C failing the probability is $F(C)R(A)R(B)$.

Total probability of one failure is

$$F(A)R(B)R(C) + F(B)R(A)R(C) + F(C)R(A)R(B).$$

67

Similarly the probability of two failures is

$$R(A)F(B)F(C) + R(B)F(A)F(C) + R(C)F(A)F(B).$$

If $R(A) = R(B) = R(C) = R$, then

$$\underset{\underset{\text{No failure}}{\uparrow}}{R^3} + \underset{\underset{\text{1 failure}}{\uparrow}}{3R^3F} + \underset{\underset{\text{2 failures}}{\uparrow}}{3F^2R} + \underset{\underset{\text{3 failures}}{\uparrow}}{F^3} = 1;$$

that is,

$$(R + F)^3 = 1.$$

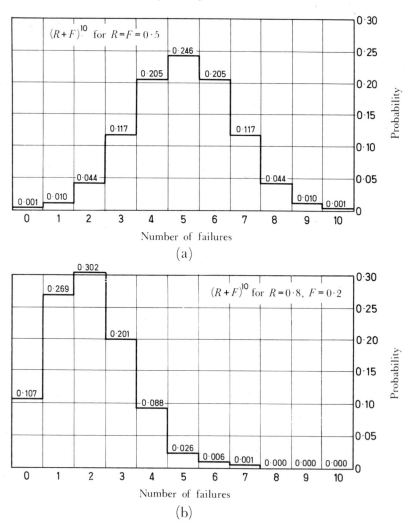

Fig. 6.4 Binomial distribution

It will become clear to the reader that this process can be continued and that the probability of a given number of failures in N pieces of equipment with the same reliability can be calculated from the expansion of

$$(R + F)^N, \qquad (6.6)$$

which is

$$(R + F)^N = R^N + NR^{N-1}F + \frac{N!}{(N-2)!\,2!}R^{N-2}F^2$$

$$+ \frac{N!}{(N-3)!\,3!}R^{N-3}F^3 + \cdots + F^N, \quad (6.7)$$

and we can use this expansion to work out the chances of any proportion failing, provided the probability of failure remains constant.

Here, R^N is the probability of no failures, $NR^{N-1}F$ that of exactly one failure, and so on.

This is called the *binomial distribution*. It can be represented in the form of a probability distribution function to show the probability of any number of failures. If the probabilities of survival and failure are equal, the distribution is symmetrical and it acquires skew as the difference between these probabilities increases. This is illustrated in Fig. 6.4, which shows the distribution drawn for 10 items and presented in histogram form when

(a) $R = 0{\cdot}5$, $F = 0{\cdot}5$
(b) $R = 0{\cdot}8$, $F = 0{\cdot}2$.

The coefficients

$$N, \quad \frac{N!}{(N-2)!\,2!}, \quad \frac{N!}{(N-3)!\,3!}, \quad \cdots$$

are the number of ways in which the particular combinations of survivals and failures can be reached. The coefficient N for the second term arises from the fact that one failure can occur in each of N components. The subsequent coefficients have a numerator $N!$, which is the total number of ways that N components can be arranged, and a denominator which gives the product of the total number of ways the survivors can be arranged with the total number of ways the failures can be arranged.

There is a short-cut method of working out the coefficients which avoids a good deal of the arithmetic. This method is known as Pascal's triangle and sets out the coefficients like this.

$(R + F)$				1		1				
$(R + F)^2$					1	2	1			
$(R + F)^3$				1	3		3	1		
$(R + F)^4$			1	4		6		4	1	
$(R + F)^5$		1	5		10		10		5	1
$(R + F)^6$	1	6	15		20		15		6	1

Each figure in the triangle is formed by adding the two figures on the previous line nearest to the figure required. These figures are the coefficient of the binomial expansion; for example,

$$(R + F)^5 = R^5 + 5R^4F + 10R^3F^2 + 10R^2\dot{F}^3 + 5RF^4 + F^5.$$

A simple example will illustrate the application of the binomial distribution. Every Christmas I hang lights on the Christmas tree; these consist of twelve coloured bulbs connected in series, and hanging them on the tree does not provide ideal conditions for their longevity. I find that, on average, I have to replace one bulb each Christmas in order to keep the tree lit. The problem is, how many spare bulbs must I keep in stock so as to be reasonably certain that I shall be able to keep the tree lit?

The probability of a bulb failing over Christmas is one in twelve or 0·083, and hence that of survival is $1 - 0·083 = 0·917$.

We can find the probabilities of any number of bulbs failing by expanding $(0·917 + 0·083)^{12}$. This gives

Probability of no failures $0·917^{12}$	$= 0·354$
Probability of one failure $12 \times 0·917^{11} \times 0·083$	$= 0·385$
Probability of two failures $66 \times 0·917^{10} \times 0·082^2$	$= 0·191$
Probability of three failures $220 \times 0·917^9 \times 0·083^3$	$= 0·0576.$

Adding these probabilities gives a probability of between none and three failures of 0·987 or a probability of 0·013 that I cannot keep the tree lit if I have three spare bulbs, a figure that I accept as reasonably remote.

The multinomial distribution

We have examined items from the point of view of either survival or failure, but we can be faced with a situation where items can fail in different ways with different consequences. For example, a system may fail in two ways, one of which results in a unit replacement while the other causes extensive damage to other equipment. Accordingly we require a method of dealing with some shades of grey as well as black and white.

As an example, we will examine a hypothetical fire-warning system where three detectors placed in different areas are connected to a single warning device. Now, suppose that each detector can fail in two ways; it can signal a warning when it should not, or it can fail to signal a warning when it should.

Let the probability of the first case (signal when it should not) be p
Let that of the second case (fail to signal when it should) be q
Let the probability that the detector will operate as it should be r.

Then, $p + q + r = 1$.

If all the detectors are assumed to be the same, we can describe the probability of all possible outcomes from the three of them by

$$(p + q + r)^3 = 1.$$

This is using the *multinomial* distribution, which is an obvious extension of the binomial. Expanding, we get

$$p^3 + 3p^2q + 3p^2r + 6pqr + 3pr^2 + 3pq^2 + 3q^2r + 3qr^2 + q^3 + r^3 = 1.$$

The first term, p^3, is the probability of all three detectors signalling a warning when they should not, $3p^2q$ is the probability of two giving a false signal and one no signal, and so on.

The multinomial distribution provides us with a convenient means of calculating the probability of a number of different events occurring in all possible combinations. It is of course necessary to be able to put values on the probability of each individual occurrence, that is p and q in the example.

The Poisson distribution

While the binomial distribution is useful if we are concerned with only a small number of individual components, it is clearly a very cumbersome tool when the number is large. Life has been made easier for us by the work of Poisson, who developed a distribution that, subject to certain limitations, is a good approximation to the binomial and has a wider application.

While it is not the purpose of this book to delve too deeply into statistical theory, which is amply covered elsewhere, the *Poisson* distribution will be developed from first principles, both as an example and in order that its use and the approximations involved may be fully appreciated.

Let the probability that n components of reliability R will survive be P_n, so that

$$P_n = R^n = (1 - F)^n.$$

Expanding this, we get

$$P_n = 1 - nF + \frac{n!\, F^2}{(n - 2)!\, 2!} - \frac{n!\, F^3}{(n - 3)!\, 3!} + \cdots$$

$$= 1 - nF + \frac{n(n - 1)F^2}{2!} - \frac{n(n - 1)(n - 2)F^3}{3!} + \cdots$$

$$= 1 - nF + \frac{n^2 F^2}{2!}\left(\frac{n - 1}{n}\right) - \frac{n^3 F^3}{3!}\left(\frac{n - 1}{n}\right)\left(\frac{n - 2}{n}\right) + \cdots$$

Provided n is a very large number, the terms in brackets approximate to unity and can be neglected, leaving

$$P_n = 1 - nF + \frac{n^2 F^2}{2!} - \frac{n^3 F^3}{3!} + \cdots. \tag{6.8}$$

We will now proceed to develop the right-hand side of this equation by another process. Expanding $(1 + 1/n)^n$, we get

$$1 + n\left(\frac{1}{n}\right) + \frac{n(n-1)}{2!}\left(\frac{1}{n}\right)^2 + \frac{n(n-1)(n-2)}{3!}\left(\frac{1}{n}\right)^3 + \cdots$$

$$= 1 + 1 + \frac{(1 - 1/n)}{2!} + \frac{(1 - 1/n)(1 - 2/n)}{3!} + \cdots$$

If n is made a very large number, all fractions having n for their denominator become very small and can be neglected giving

$$1 + 1 + \frac{1}{2!} + \frac{1}{3!} + \cdots,$$

which can be written

$$\frac{1}{0!} + \frac{1}{1!} + \frac{1}{2!} + \frac{1}{3!} + \cdots = 2 \cdot 7183 \cdots$$

This is used as the base for the natural logarithm and is denoted by the symbol e. Since

$$e \simeq \left(1 + \frac{1}{n}\right)^n,$$

n being large,

$$e^{-x} \simeq \left(1 + \frac{1}{n}\right)^{-nx}$$

Expanding, we get

$$e^{-x} = 1 - nx\left(\frac{1}{n}\right) + \frac{nx(nx-1)}{2!}\left(\frac{1}{n}\right)^2$$

$$- \frac{nx(nx-1)(nx-2)}{3!}\left(\frac{1}{n}\right)^3 + \cdots$$

$$= 1 - x + \frac{x^2}{2!} - \frac{x^3}{3!} + \cdots$$

Replacing x by nF gives

$$e^{-nF} \simeq 1 - nF + \frac{n^2 F^2}{2!} - \frac{n^3 F^3}{3!} + \cdots,$$

the right-hand side of which is the same as (6.8), so we can write

$$P_n \simeq (1 - F)^n = e^{-nF} \tag{6.9}$$

provided n is a large number.

The next step is to apply this equation to the remaining terms of the binomial distribution. Taking the second term, where there are $n - 1$ survivors and one failure, we have

$$P_{n-1} = nR^{n-1}F$$

$$= nF(1 - F)^{n-1}$$

$$= nF(1 - F)^n \frac{1}{1 - F}$$

$$= nF e^{-nF} \frac{1}{1 - F}.$$

The third term can be treated similarly:

$$P_{n-2} = \frac{n!}{(n - 2)! \, 2!} R^{n-2}F^2$$

$$= \frac{n(n - 1)F^2}{2!} (1 - F)^{n-2}$$

$$= \frac{n^2F^2(1 - f)^n}{2!} \left(\frac{1}{1 - F}\right)^2 \left(\frac{n - 1}{n}\right)$$

$$= n^2F^2 e^{-nF} \left(\frac{1}{1 - F}\right)^2 \left(\frac{n - 1}{n}\right).$$

Provided n is very large and F is very small, the terms in brackets approximate to unity and can be neglected.

The terms of the binomial distribution can now be written

$$e^{-nF} + nFe^{-nF} + \frac{n^2F^2}{2!} e^{-nF} + \cdots = e^{-nF} \left(1 + nF + \frac{n^2F^2}{2!} + \ldots,\right)$$

(6.10)

where the first term gives the chance of no failures, the second that of one failure, the third that of two failures and so on. The assumptions are that n is large and F is small, which is almost always the case in practice. No appreciable error is introduced by n being small, and F must have a value that would normally be quite unacceptable before the error becomes marked.

It will be seen that the first term, representing no failures, can be transformed into the negative exponential expression $e^{-\lambda t}$ by the substitution of n for t and F for λ.

Where we are concerned with the probability of a specific number of events such as failure, which we will call y, we can write

$$P(y) = \frac{e^{-nF}(nF)^y}{y!}.$$

(6.11)

This is the Poisson distribution, and since we assume that F is small, it is always a skew distribution.

In many cases, we do not know the values of n and F, but we do know nF, which is the average number of failures. It is common practice to denote this average, that is the number we expect, by m and write the equation as

$$P(y) = \frac{e^{-m}m^y}{y!}. \qquad (6.12)$$

Values of $P(y)$ for different values of nF are given in statistical tables, and to make life even easier, a chart has been made available where the probability of a given number of failures or less occurring can be read off for values of nF. This is known as the Poisson probability chart and a copy is given in Fig. 14.5. It is recommended that anyone concerned with reliability calculations should arm themselves with a pad of these charts.

Values of nF ($= a$) are given on the bottom scale, which is a logarithmic one, and the probability on the left-hand scale which is in the form of a normal probability scale. The number of failures are given by the curved lines on the chart, each one of which represents the maximum number of failures that correspond with appropriate values of P and nF. On the chart, the number of failures are given the notation c. Thus,

$$c = 1 \text{ gives } 1 - e^{-nF}$$

$$c = 2 \text{ gives } 1 - e^{-nF}(1 + nF)$$

$$c = 3 \text{ gives } 1 - e^{-nF}\left(1 + nF + \frac{n^2F^2}{2!}\right)$$

and so on.

To find the probability of exactly three failures we read off the probability of three or less, $c = 3$, and subtract the probability of two or less, $c = 2$.

Examples of the application of the Poisson distribution On a certain component, experience shows that the failure rate is constant and averages 0·010 per 1000 hours. Only two spares are available and there is no prospect of obtaining any more for six months, during which time we expect to use the equipment for 50,000 hours. We wish to know the chance of some equipment being out of use because of spares shortage.

Probability of three failures

$$= e^{-\lambda t}\frac{\lambda^3 t^3}{3!}$$

$$= \exp\left(-\frac{0\cdot010 \times 50,000}{1000}\right)\frac{(0\cdot010 \times 50,000/1000)^3}{6}$$

$$= 0\cdot0127.$$

In the same way the probability of four failures is found to be 0·0015. It is not necessary to explore the probability of greater numbers of failures owing to their obvious remoteness. Hence, the probability of our requiring more than our two spares is

$$0·0126 + 0·0016 \approx 0·014$$

which is what we wanted to know.

Besides applying this method to numbers of pieces of equipment, we can apply it to an individual item. For example, suppose we have a component which has had to be replaced twice in a particular system, while the general replacement rate of this component is fairly low. The question arises: is this due to chance or is there something wrong with the system?

Assume $\lambda = 0·1$ per 1000 hours. On the suspect system the component was replaced twice in 2000 hours.

Probability of 2 failures in 2000 hours

$$= e^{-\lambda t} \frac{\lambda^2 t^2}{2!}$$

$$= \exp\left(-\frac{0·1 \times 2000}{1000}\right) \frac{(0·1 \times 2000/1000)^2}{2}$$

$$= 0·016.$$

Since there is only a 0·016 probability of two components both failing in 2000 hours it would be worth while to investigate the system.

Confidence limits

We have seen how, given an expected number of failures, we can calculate the probability of some other number occurring. Clearly this statement can be turned round: given a probability of failure, we can calculate the maximum and minimum number of failures that are encompassed by a given probability. In this way we arrive at *confidence limits*.

If we spin a coin ten times we can expect to get, on the average, five heads and five tails, but in fact this event is far from certain. It is however comparatively unlikely that we shall get ten heads or ten tails. Using the binomial distribution, we can work out the probability of any combination of heads and tails occurring, and the result is shown in Fig. 6.5. The probability of each occurrence is shown and by adding these probabilities (each spin is mutually exclusive) we can assess the probability of not getting more or less heads than any specified number.

We see from the diagram that the probability of getting more than 7 heads is 0·055, this being the sum of the probabilities of 8, 9, and 10 heads. We could also say that the probability of getting at least 7 heads = $1 - 0·055 = 0·945$, or alternatively that we have 0·945 confidence that

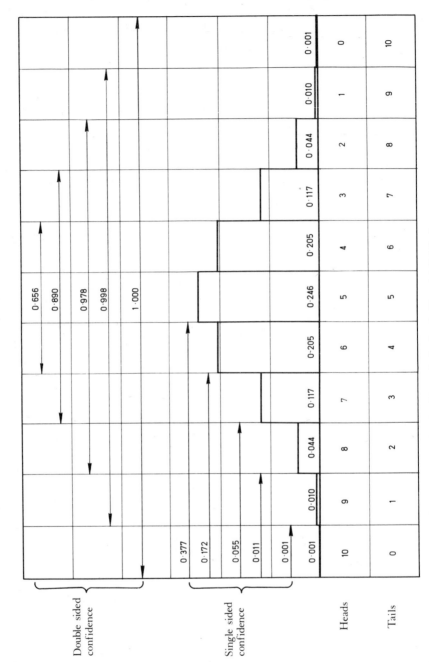

Fig. 6.5 Confidence limits for the binomial distribution

we shall not get more than 7 heads. Confidence is usually expressed as a percentage, and in our example, 7 represents the upper 94·5 per cent confidence limit. Similarly, 3 represents the lower 94·5 per cent confidence limit. The band between 3 and 7 is termed the *confidence band*, and represents a $1 - 2 \times 0·055$ probability. That is, we have 89 per cent confidence that the result will fall in this band.

In this example, we have confidence limits that refer to one end of the distribution only, being confident that not more than a number of events will occur or alternatively not less than a number of events will occur. These are termed single-sided or single-tail confidence limits. We also have confidence limits giving the probability that the number of events will not be either greater or less than defined numbers. These are called double-sided or two-tail limits.

Figure 6.6 illustrates the meaning of these definitions. The area of the tails of the distributions outside the confidence limits is called the *level of significance* and is given the symbol α. It will be appreciated that it is particularly important to state whether single-sided or double-sided confidence limits are being used, as in the former case the confidence is $1 - \alpha$ and in the latter $1 - 2\alpha$. The use of confidence limits makes the statistical interpretation of reliability results much more meaningful.

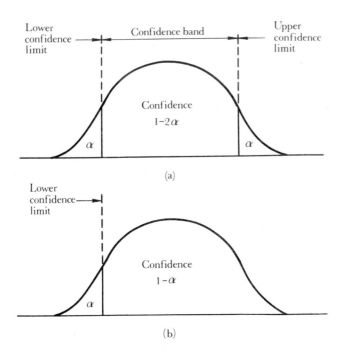

**Fig. 6.6 (a) Double-sided or two-tailed confidence limits.
(b) Single-sided or single-tailed confidence limits**

Confidence limits for the binomial distribution Our introductory example showed that confidence limits could be derived from the binomial distribution, and we will now examine this further.

First, taking the case where no failures have occurred, we can write:

Probability of getting failures

$$= 1 - \text{probability of no failures} = 1 - R^N.$$

The confidence we have in the reliability is equal to the probability of failure given that no failures have actually occurred.

This is illustrated diagrammatically in Fig. 6.7, which is in the same form as Fig. 6.6. As N increases, R^N decreases, and the confidence level moves to the left, increasing the confidence. We can accordingly write

$$\text{Confidence} = C = 1 - R^N. \tag{6.13}$$

We can set the level of confidence and work out values for R with any given value of N.

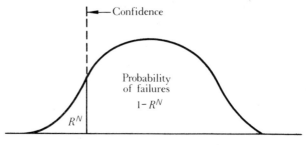

Fig. 6.7

As an example, suppose we wish to know the reliability we have established, with 90 per cent confidence, following the successful conclusion of twenty tests. From (6.13), we have

$$0.9 = 1 - R^{20},$$

$$\therefore R = \sqrt[20]{0.1} = 0.89.$$

If we get one failure we can establish our confidence in the same way, but now we must use the first two terms of the binomial expansion and set the confidence equal to one or less failures. The equation now becomes

$$C = 1 - \left[R^N + NR^{N-1}(1 - R) \right]. \tag{6.14}$$

In the same way, equations for the confidence in R can be written for any given number of failures.

These equations can be solved for R only by iterative methods but, as may be expected, they have been worked out and the results published in the form of charts and tables.* For general reliability purposes charts are quite accurate enough and are more convenient to use than tables.

Calculation of rank values   Equations (6.13), (6.14), and the similar equations that embrace the subsequent terms of the binomial expansion, provide us with an accurate method of calculating the rank values that we used to calculate the probabilities needed for the ranking method for plotting mortality curves. For calculating the median life rank value C is set at 0·50.

For example, given a test where ten components were tested to failure, the median rank for the first failure can be calculated from

$$0·50 = 1 - R^{10}$$

$$\therefore R = \sqrt[10]{0·50} = 0·9330.$$

$$\text{Median rank} = 1 - 0·9330 = 0·0670.$$

Using the alternative method of calculating rank values, eq. (2.3), we obtain

$$\frac{1 - 0·3}{10 + 0·4} = 0·0677, \text{ which is a good approximation.}$$

Confidence limits for the Poisson distribution   We can use the terms of the Poisson instead of the binomial to calculate confidence limits. In this case we have the restriction that N must be a large number.

Given the number of failures we expect, NF, we can read the number that we may get with any degree of confidence, that is the confidence limit, directly from the Poisson probability chart (Fig. 6.8). If the reader does an exercise comparing the values he obtains from the Poisson with those given by the binomial he will find that the difference when $N = 100$ is small and that the values are almost identical when N reaches 1000.

Where N is large and indeterminable, the Poisson distribution can be useful for determining the confidence limits. Let us take as an example the case of some aircraft equipment that has been giving trouble. We assume that the trouble is not time related because, if this were so, we should have to take the age of the equipment into account. It takes a month to repair the equipment when it fails, so we require sufficient stand-by sets to cater for the number of failures experienced in a month. We are prepared to take a $\frac{1}{20}$ chance that we shall not have enough standby sets, since these are expensive. The average number of failures per month over the last few months has been 15.

* See, for example, Burington and May, *Handbook of Probability and Statistics with Tables*, McGraw-Hill (1953).

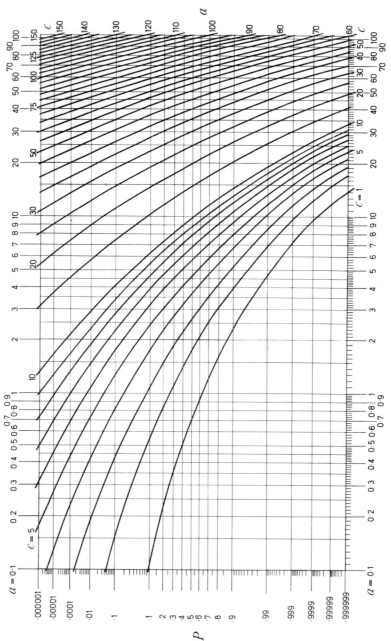

Fig. 6.8 Probability curves showing Poisson's exponential summation

$$P = 1 - \left[1 + \frac{a}{1!} + \frac{a^2}{2!} + \cdots + \frac{a^{c-1}}{(c-1)!} \right] e^{-n}$$

for the probability P that an event occurs at least c times in a large group of trials for which the average number of occurrences is a. A scale proportional to the normal probability integral is

The problem can now be stated as, if $NF = 15$, what is the single-sided upper limit for 95 per cent (19 in 20) confidence? From the Poisson probability chart, we find that the lines for $NF = 15$ and $P = 0.05$ intersect at between $c = 22$ and $c = 23$. Accordingly we require 23 stand-by sets if we are to avoid a greater risk than one in twenty of not having spares available.

Limits for mortality curves

When we consider confidence limits for mortality curves, we can approach the problem in two ways. We can assume that the type of distribution we have selected is correct, and base our calculations on the parameters that arise from this distribution, or we can assume nothing, and calculate confidence-limit curves from our original data. In this book we will confine ourselves to the second approach. Firstly, because the calculations involved in estimating confidence limits from parameters is involved, it cannot be done satisfactorily for the Weibull distribution, which is complicated by the three parameters γ, β and η, and some assumption has to be made regarding one of them, usually γ. Secondly because, in principle, it is usually unwise to make any assumptions unless this is essential.

An exception is where a constant failure rate can be assumed because we are considering the failures of items over a period of calendar time during which the lives of the items will vary. In such a case we are concerned with the confidence limits we can put on the overall failure rate or M.T.B.F. Confidence limits for M.T.B.F. are normally calculated using the chi-squared distribution and we will study this later on. For other cases we use the binomial distribution, which, as we have seen, derives entirely from first principles.

We must now consider the case where parts, originally exposed to failure, are removed from test or service for reasons other than failure. Some adjustment to N or n is required or the confidence limits will be wrongly estimated. When we calculated mortality curves by proportion methods, we increased n to compensate for parts removed before failure, but this procedure, if applied to confidence-limit calculations, would lead to an over-estimation of the upper limit. We must accordingly adopt the alternative procedure of estimating reduced values of n for each point we calculate on the confidence-limit curves.

Let $N'(t)$ be the number surviving at time t, and
$n'(t)$ be the number of failures from a population $N'(t) + n'(t)$ that would occur up to time t.

If we can evaluate $n'(t)$, we can obtain the confidence limits from the charts by putting $n'(t) = n$ and $N'(t) + n'(t) = N$.

Now

$$F(t) = \frac{n'(t)}{N'(t) + n'(t)}, \tag{6.15}$$

so that, provided we can make an approximate estimation of $N'(t) + n'(t)$, we can calculate $n'(t)$ with a reasonable degree of accuracy.

Where $N'(t)$ is large, it is sufficient to estimate $N'(t) + n'(t)$ by guess because, provided $n'(t)$ is relatively small, its value calculated from eq. (6.15) will not be seriously in error. Where doubt exists, reference to the charts will indicate whether a more accurate estimation than a guess is warranted. Should greater accuracy be required, the method of approximate estimation set out in Table 6.1 may be used. The method may be explained as follows.

The second row of the table gives values of $N'(t)$, and the third row a guessed estimate of $n'(t)$ expressed as $1 + x$, where the 1 relates to the failure that occurred at the value of t for the particular column, and the x to the number of failures guessed to have occurred at earlier hours had no additional items been previously exposed to failure.

Suppose we wish to estimate the value of $n'(t_4)$. Three failures have occurred previously; we guess the number that would have occurred if additional items had not been exposed as $x = 2$. We give each of the earlier failures a value of $\frac{2}{3}$ relative to the number exposed at t_4.

Considering the failure at t_1, at this time the 18 that survived to t_4 would have been $18 + 3 \times \frac{2}{3}$, the failure at t_1, t_2, and t_3 each being regarded as $\frac{2}{3}$ of a failure. We now proportion the failure at t_1 by $(18 + 3 \times \frac{2}{3})/40 = 0·50$. The square referred to is shown in Table 6.1 in bold outline.

In this way, each previous failure is proportioned and the sum of these provides a second estimate of $n'(t)$ and an estimate of $N'(t) + n'(t)$. The method is seen to be an approximate one, but it is accurate enough for practical purposes.

Having made an estimate of $N'(t) + n'(t)$, we can introduce the calculation of $n'(t)$ and the confidence limits into a tabulation for the calculation of a mortality curve. Taking the data used in Table 6.1 as the example, the mortality-curve calculation with confidence limits is set out in Table 6.2.

It will be seen that the mortality curve has been calculated by proportion methods. This is necessary if eq. (6.15) is to hold good. It will be appreciated that the confidence limits calculated from the terms of the binomial expansion are properly associated with points on mortality curves that have been plotted at the median rank values so that if the values of $N'(t) + n'(t)$ and $n'(t)$ given in Tables 6.1 and 6.2 are applied to obtain the confidence limits, the answers will be different from those that would properly correspond to a median-ranked mortality curve. This difference is negligible, except on the upper confidence-limit curve, over the range of the first five failures.

Table 6.1 Estimation of $N'(t) + n'(t)$

		t_1	t_2	t_3	t_4	t_5
$N'(t)$		39	34	26	17	11
$n'(t)$ First estimate		$1 + 0$	$1 + 1$	$1 + 2$	$1 + 2$	$1 + 2$
Exposed	*Failed*					
40	1	1	$1 \times \dfrac{35+1}{40} = 0.9$	$1 \times \dfrac{27+2}{40} = 0.725$	$1 \times \dfrac{18+3 \times \frac{2}{3}}{40} = 0.50$	$1 \times \dfrac{12+4 \times \frac{2}{4}}{40} = 0.35$
35	1	—	—	$1 \times \dfrac{27+1}{35} = 0.80$	$1 \times \dfrac{18+2 \times \frac{2}{3}}{35} = 0.57$	$1 \times \dfrac{12+3 \times \frac{2}{4}}{35} = 0.385$
27	1	—	—	1	$1 \times \dfrac{18+1 \times \frac{2}{3}}{27} = 0.69$	$1 \times \dfrac{12+2 \times \frac{2}{4}}{27} = 0.48$
18	1	—	—	—	1	$1 \times \dfrac{12+1 \times \frac{2}{4}}{18} = 0.695$
12	1	—	—	—	—	1
$n'(t)$ Second estimate		1	1·9	2·525	2·755	2·910
$N'(t) + n'(t)$		40	35·9	28·525	19·755	13·912

Table 6.2 Calculation of confidence limits for a mortality curve

(1)	(2)	(3)	(4)	(5)	(6)	(7)	(8)	(9)	(10)	(11)	(12)
Life to failure (hours)	Number of failures	Number exposed	Proportion failed	Proportion survived	$R(t)$	$F(t)$	$n'(t)$ (estimated)	$N'(t) + n'(t)$ (estimated)	$n'(t)$ (calculated)	Lower 90 per cent confidence	Upper 90 per cent confidence
1004	1	40	0·025	0·975	0·975	0·025	1	40	1·00	0·00125	0·064 0·074
1521	1	35	0·028	0·972	0·948	0·052	1·9	35·9	1·87	0·0075	0·120 0·125
2167	1	27	0·037	0·963	0·913	0·087	2·52	28·5	2·48	0·023	0·185 0·180
2590	1	18	0·055	0·945	0·862	0·138	2·75	19·8	2·73	0·033	0·270
3672	1	12	0·083	0·917	0·791	0·209	2·91	13·9	2·90	0·055	0·390

7

The initial strength and failure distributions of parts under constant duty: the extreme-value and log extreme-value distributions

The previous argument that the initial strength distribution was normal was demonstrated by laboratory test results on small specimens. When we consider actual components, the introduction of additional factors can considerably modify the form of the initial strength and failure distributions obtained from laboratory tests, and result in a reduction in the spread of lives to failure. The additional factors we must consider are variations in the quality and strength over the portions of the parts that are exposed to failure.

As an illustration, we will take a case of fatigue failures originating at the blade fixing points of a turbine disc. The disc cycles between standstill and high speed each time the engine is started and stopped, imposing a stress cycle on the blade fixing points. We will regard all these points as being equally stressed under the high-speed running condition.

When a fatigue crack occurs, it can be expected to originate at the weakest fixing point. The weakness is occasioned by the longest inclusion, worst tool mark, or other imperfection, coupled with the strength of the material at the particular point. The larger the number of blades, the greater the number of possible points of weakness. By contrast, a laboratory fatigue specimen has a small area exposed to failure, and this is carefully controlled to minimize surface imperfections, or has a controlled notch so that the number of points of weakness is minimal.

There is clearly a relationship between the number of blades and the probability of an imperfection of a given size.

Now the strength of the individual fixing points in any one disc will have a distribution, and for the purposes of our study we will assume that this is normal. When it is considered that this strength is composed of a number of factors, including material strength and surface finish, it will be seen that the central limit theorem becomes applicable, and the assumption of a normal distribution is sensible.

With the assumption of a normal distribution, we will examine graphically the relationship between the number of blades and the probability of a point of low strength, the mathematics being rather complicated. Figure 7.1 shows a normal distribution drawn on probability paper. For simplicity, the line has been drawn so that the standard deviation is one. The median rank values of the lowest probability relative to various sample sizes are shown, and from the graph we can read off the expected number of

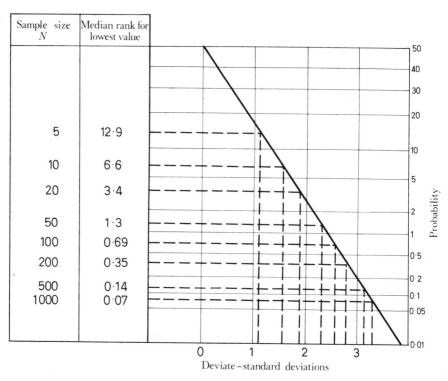

Fig. 7.1

standard deviations that correspond to the lowest value that is expected to occur in different sample sizes. In Fig. 7.2, the results of the exercise are plotted as the expected deviate, in terms of standard deviations, against sample size or areas exposed to failure N.

If we relate Fig. 7.2 to our turbine blade example, we see that if we have, say, 100 blades, we can expect to encounter one blade fixing point that is weaker than the average to the extent of 2·60. Now it is unlikely that it will be exactly 2·60, but it will be of this order. The dotted lines shown in the figure have been calculated to show the band within which the lowest value of strength can be expected to fall 9 times out of 10. The method by which these lines have been calculated will be understood when we examine confidence limits. If the strength distribution is not normal, the same process can be carried out and will yield generally similar results.

Figure 7.2 demonstrates that as the number of areas exposed to failure increases, the variation in the expected strength of the weakest point decreases. This result might be foreseen without the aid of statistics.

If we now consider a large number of discs, each one of these will have a distribution of the strength of the blade fixing points and there will be an overall distribution that embraces the strength of all the points on all discs.

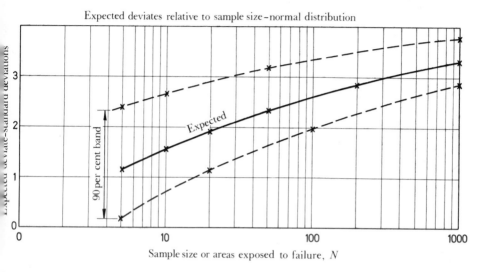

Fig. 7.2

A diagrammatic representation of the situation is shown in Fig. 7.3.

Since the probability of failure relative to individual discs is approaching the lower end of the embraced distributions, we see that the overall scatter in lives to failure between discs is related to the variation between discs and the number of blades per disc.

An example will show how rapidly the variation in life to failure reduces with an increase in the number exposed to failure. For this example we will take a series of tests on ball bearings which resulted in ball failure, these tests all being run at the same condition.

The mortality curve for the bearings is shown plotted on Weibull paper in Fig. 7.4. We will now make the assumption that one ball in each bearing failed and the rest were surviving at the time of failure. With this assumption, we can plot the mortality curve for balls, there being nine balls in each bearing. This is also shown in Fig. 7.4.

While 50 per cent of bearings are expected to fail by 2.7×10^7 revolutions, 50 per cent of balls would require 12.5×10^7 revolutions. The difference in the ratio

$$\frac{\text{revolutions to 50 per cent failure}}{\text{revolutions to 1 per cent failure}}$$

is marked, and is about 2 : 1.

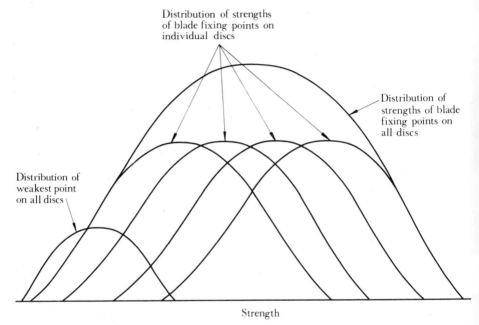

Distribution of strengths of blade fixing points on individual discs

Distribution of strengths of blade fixing points on all discs

Distribution of weakest point on all discs

Strength

Fig. 7.3

It can be seen that, when we come to consider the forms of strength and life-to-failure distributions of parts, we must take account of the number of points or the area of the part that is exposed to failure. If there are many weak points, the resulting failure distribution is not log normal. It will be restricted at the high-life end because the weakest point in each specimen fails first, so that those at the stronger end of the distribution never reach the life at which they would fail.

In the case of our turbine disc example we have a large number of possible weak points and the normal and log normal distributions are no longer applicable to the strength and failure distributions. We require a distribution that will define the probability of the weakest point, given that there are many weak points and that these may reasonably be expected to be normally distributed. We accordingly introduce the *extreme-value distribution*.

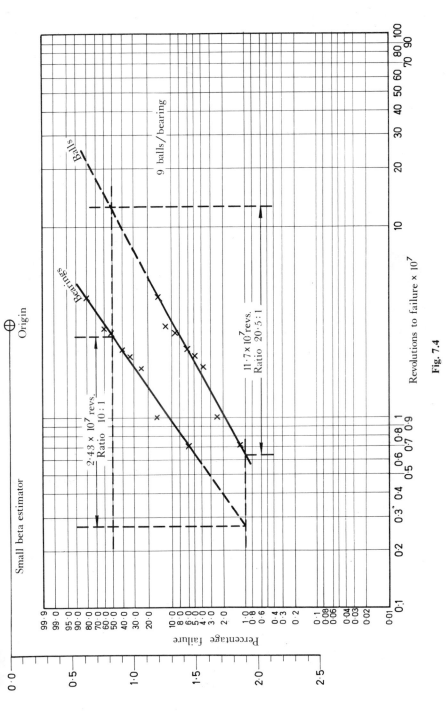

Fig. 7.4

89

The extreme-value distribution

It is not proposed to go into the theory that lies behind the extreme-value distribution, which is of only academic interest to reliability engineers. Any reader who is interested is recommended to read E. J. Gumbel's writings on the subject. We shall confine ourselves to the principles involved, the uses to which the distribution can be put, and the way it can be applied.

The extreme-value distribution is a distribution of the probabilities of values being exceeded. We can also say that it is the distribution of the largest (or smallest) value for a large number of samples. The cumulative function is

$$F = e^{-e^{-y}}, \qquad (7.1)$$

where $y = a(x - \bar{x})$, a being a measure of dispersion.

When we studied the normal distribution, we saw that the probability of the value of x being exceeded could be related to $(x - \bar{x})/\sigma$. It will be seen that $a(x - \bar{x})$ corresponds to the $(x - \bar{x})/\sigma$ of the normal distribution.

The graph of $F = e^{-e^{-y}}$ on log log versus linear paper is a straight line when y is plotted as the linear co-ordinate. Accordingly this type of paper is called extreme-value probability paper, and it is illustrated in Fig. 7.5. The cumulative probability scale is the same as that on Weibull paper, except that it is annotated in the reverse direction. A scale giving the inverse of the cumulative probability values is given at the top of the paper. This is called the *return period*, since it indicates the number of events between the return of a particular value.

We can use the extreme-value distribution to plot either the probability of being less than the life (or other parameter) or the probability of being greater than these values; this is illustrated in Fig. 7.5. In other words we can use the cumulative probability scale for either $F(t)$ or $R(t)$. It will be seen that the distribution must be skewed; a glance at the probability scale on the paper will confirm this. We must plot our distribution with reference to its direction of skewness if we are to obtain the best fit to a straight line on extreme-value paper. Where a distribution is skewed towards the high values, we plot the probability of being greater than the scale values or $R(t)$, and where it is skewed towards the low values, the probability of being less than or $F(t)$.

The applications of the extreme-value distribution We introduced the extreme-value distribution to describe the probability of the weakest of a number of weak points whose strength was reasonably normally distributed. The sort of distribution that we require is a normal distribution that is compressed at the high-value side.

The reader can demonstrate for himself that this requirement is met by the extreme-value distribution, if he is prepared to carry out the following

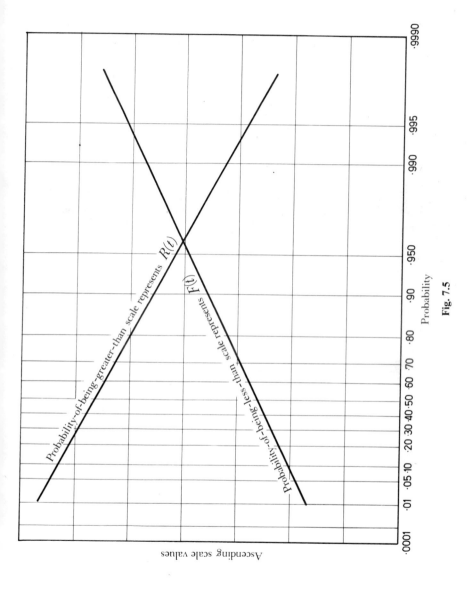

Fig. 7.5

exercise. First, take a normal distribution and divide it into equal areas, each representing an equal probability. The value corresponding to each increment is then taken from the base scale. This can be done quite easily by means of a piece of normal probability paper or by reference to tables. The values represent the strengths of a normally distributed strength distribution. Write each value on a small piece of paper, shuffle the pieces well and select a sample, representing one part. The lowest value in the sample is the strength of the part. Return the sample to the pile, re-shuffle and take another sample. To get a good result at least twenty samples should be taken, the more the better. The lowest values from each sample are then plotted on extreme-value probability paper, using the probability scale as the probability of their having a strength less than the strength scale values—that is, the line should slope down to the bottom right-hand corner. The reader should find that he produces a reasonable extreme-value distribution with a sample size as small as two.

The results of this exercise as performed by the author for various sample sizes is shown in Fig. 7.6. The normal distribution from which the samples were taken is also shown.

The extreme-value distribution also has applications in a number of other circumstances. It will have become clear to the reader that probability distributions are usually described by exponential expressions, so that we can assume that the probability distribution for initial strength M_0 is of the form $e^{-f(M_0)}$, where f denotes 'function of'. We can write the probability of a particular value of M_0 as

$$P = e^{-f(M_0)}.$$

If we compare this equation with the one obtained for the negative exponential distribution, eq. (3.1), we see that it will plot as a straight line on log linear paper when the function of M_0 is linear:

$$\log_e \frac{1}{P} = \text{linear function of } M_0.$$

Hence, if M_0 occurs at random and can be described by the negative exponential distribution,

$$P = e^{-cM_0},$$

c being a constant.

Where the duty is constant, we have shown that the time to failure is a function of $\log_e M_0$, so we can say

$$\log_e \log_e \frac{1}{P} = \text{linear function of time to failure } (M_0 \text{ occurring at random}).$$

This equation describes the probability scales on extreme-value paper, so where the strength is randomly distributed we expect the failure distri-

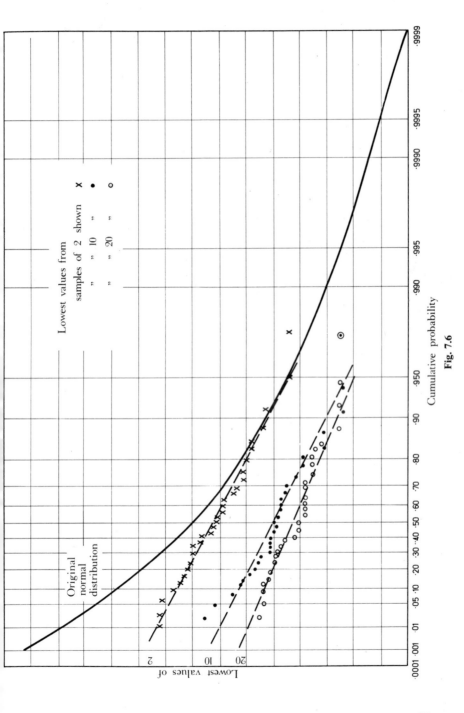

Fig. 7.6

Cumulative probability

Lowest values of

Lowest values from
samples of 2 shown   ×
        „   „ 10   „   ●
        „   „ 20   „   ○

Original
normal
distribution

bution to appear as a straight line on this paper. Some test results behave in this way and an example of fatigue-test results plotted on extreme-value probability paper is given in Fig. 7.7.

We can also take the case where the function of M_0 is a log function or approximates to one:

$$P = e^{-c \log_e M_0},$$

in which case we can say

$$\log_e \log_e \frac{1}{P} = \text{linear function of } M_0,$$

and the strength distribution appears as a straight line on extreme-value probability paper.

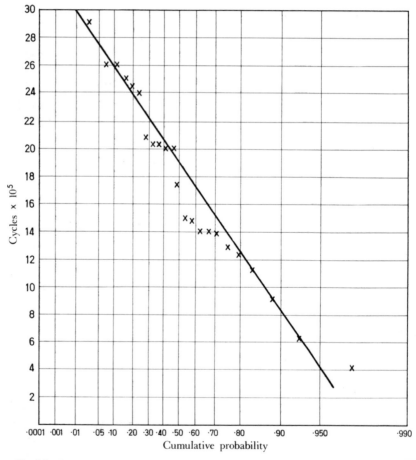

Fig. 7.7 **Example of fatigue-test results on extreme-value paper (rotating bend tests on an alloy steel)**

In discussing normal strength distributions the author included the proviso that there must be no dominant controlling parameter for the normal distribution to appear. Where there is such a parameter the resulting strength must be dependent on its value, which in many cases can be appropriately described by the extreme-value distribution. We thus have a distribution that describes many departures from the general case, particularly if one of the controlling factors is dominant.

The log extreme-value distribution

When we come to consider the lives to failure of parts whose strength distribution is of the extreme-value type, we require to put the extreme-value distribution on a log base to convert the strength distribution into a life to failure distribution. We accordingly introduce the *log extreme-value distribution*.

We will examine the log extreme-value distribution by taking the expression for $R(t)$ and showing that this meets this requirement. We start with

$$R(t) = 1 - \exp[-(\alpha/t)^\beta], \tag{7.2}$$

where α is a scale parameter, β is a shape parameter. Then,

$$F(t) = 1 - R(t) = \exp[-(\alpha/t)^\beta]. \tag{7.3}$$

From eq. (1.4),

$$f(t) = \frac{dF(t)}{dt} = \frac{\beta\alpha^\beta}{t^{\beta+1}} \exp\left[-\left(\frac{\alpha}{t}\right)^\beta\right], \tag{7.4}$$

and from eq. (1.5),

$$Z(t) = \frac{f(t)}{R(t)} = \frac{\beta\alpha^\beta}{t^{\beta+1}} \left(\frac{1}{1 - \exp[-(\alpha/t)^\beta]}\right) \exp\left[-\left(\frac{\alpha}{t}\right)^\beta\right]. \tag{7.5}$$

We derive the equation for log extreme-value probability paper as follows:

$$R(t) = 1 - \exp[-(\alpha/t)^\beta]$$

$$F(t) = \exp[-(\alpha/t)^\beta]$$

$$\frac{1}{F(t)} = \exp[(\alpha/t)^\beta]$$

$$\log_e \frac{1}{F(t)} = (\alpha/t)^\beta$$

$$\log_e \log_e \frac{1}{F(t)} = \beta \log_e \alpha - \beta \log_e t. \tag{7.6}$$

This is similar to the Weibull equation, (6.5), except that the left-hand side is $\log_e \log_e [1/F(t)]$ instead of $\log_e \log_e 1/[1 - F(t)]$. It is thus seen that log extreme-value probability paper is the same as Weibull paper except that the values of $F(t)$ on the latter are replaced by $R(t)$. The log extreme-value distribution is also different from the Weibull in as much as it is centred at

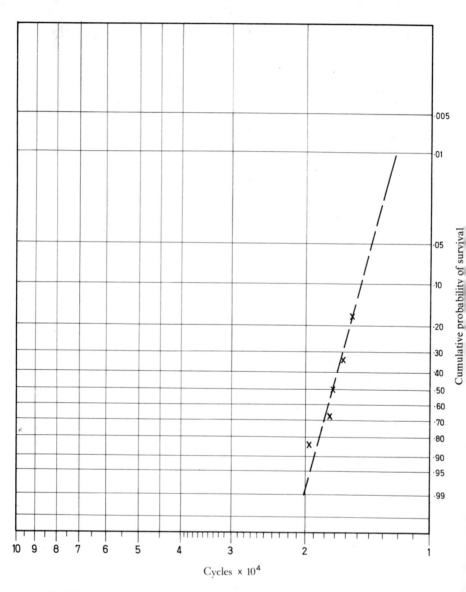

Cycles × 10^4

Fig. 7.8   Example of log extreme-value (log double exponential) probability paper with plot of turbine disc firtree failures at constant stress

the mode which is usually the 37 per cent probability point and not at zero, so that no datum adjustment is required.

An example of log extreme-value probability paper is shown in Fig. 7.8, from which it will be observed that it is simply extreme-value paper with the linear scale replaced by a log one, which is what we required for plotting our life-to-failure distribution under constant duty conditions.

The curve shown plotted in Fig. 7.8 is taken from data relative to the

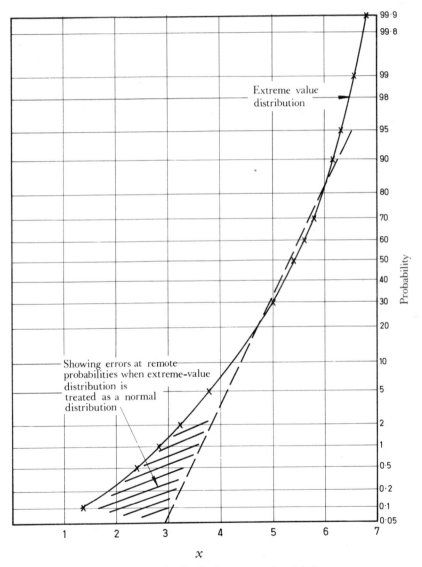

Fig. 7.9   Extreme-value distribution on normal probability paper

failures of broached firtree blade slots in turbine discs when tested under constant cyclic conditions. This is the example on which our argument leading to the extreme-value distribution was based. It is pertinent to note that there is a very small scatter in lives to failure, the ratio of cycles between 1 per cent and 99 per cent probability of failure being of the order of 2·5 to 1.

The normal and extreme-value distributions compared

Taking the general case where the initial strength of a part arises from a number of variable factors, we have established that the distribution of this strength should follow the normal distribution where there is a single point of weakness, and the extreme-value distribution where there are several points of weakness, the latter being particularly applicable to fatigue strength. We can regard these two distributions as limiting forms, assuming no special influence is present, and it is pertinent to compare them.

A plot of a normal distribution on extreme-value paper has been shown in Fig. 7.6.

In Fig. 7.9 an extreme-value distribution is shown plotted on normal probability paper. It will be appreciated that it could be mistaken for a normal distribution. The dashed line in Fig. 7.9 shows that there is little departure from the normal between 5 per cent and 95 per cent, an area that frequently contains the points available for plotting. Such departure could reasonably be put down to chance or experimental error. As the figure shows, the assumption of a normal distribution instead of an extreme-value could lead to an underestimate at the remoter probabilities.

In many of the examples that have been quoted, there are sufficient data to establish that the form of the distribution was normal or log normal beyond reasonable doubt; in others the normal or log normal has been assumed but some of these may have been extreme-value distributions or somewhere between the two.

When the reader is trying to establish a distribution from a limited amount of data, and finds it plots reasonably well on normal or log normal probability paper he is advised to consider whether an extreme-value or log extreme-value distribution is more likely in the particular circumstances before he attempts any extrapolation.

8

Some further considerations regarding distributions of fatigue-test results and minimum fatigue life

The form of the fatigue curve

While this is not a book about fatigue, it is relevant to give some brief consideration to the form of the stress/cycles-to-failure curve since, in some cases, that can influence the distribution of fatigue strength.

We can consider this curve in terms of strain rather than stress and replace the alternating stress scale by a scale of the range of strain. Manson and others have shown that if the log of the strain range is plotted against cycles to failure the log strain-range/log cycles-to-failure curve is the summation of two straight lines, one representing the fatigue life characteristic in the region where the strain results in elastic deformation of the material, and the other where the strain produces a permanent deformation and which can be termed the plastic strain range. Both lines are extrapolated over the whole strain range.

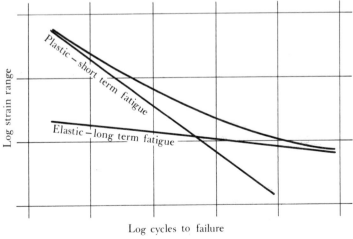

Log cycles to failure

Fig. 8.1

The concept is illustrated in Fig. 8.1. It is seen that the curve becomes asymptotic with the lines representing the elastic and plastic fatigue characteristics as the strain is increased or decreased relative to the point where change-over occurs. The portion of the curve where the plastic characteristic is predominant represents short-term fatigue, and the other portion long-term fatigue.

We have previously postulated the relationship $1/D = b \log_e N + K$, with the warning that this should be used only over a small range of duty. It will be seen that this is reasonably compatible with the curve shown in Fig. 8.1, provided it is applied within either the elastic or plastic strain ranges.

Distribution of test results

Turning to the distributions of fatigue-test results, we note that two arguments have been advanced. The first is that, due to a normal distribution of initial strength, the failure distribution is log normal. The second is that failure occurs at the weakest spot, which in the case of parts leads to the log extreme-value distribution. The reader may question whether the second argument should be applied rather than that of normally distributed strength. In fact both arguments are correct as further study will show. A large number of fatigue tests on small specimens have produced distributions that are undoubtedly log normal, and the cycles to failure must sensibly be regarded as being related to some measure of the average strength of the specimens.

The tests carried out by Ellison and Brook, where the true elastic limit was measured at stages during the fatigue tests, confirm this supposition. The remaining fatigue life is found to relate to the true elastic limit, which was a measure closer to the average strength at the surface than that at one point on the surface.

We can reasonably assume that the cycles to failure is a function of the strength of the material that surrounds that point of fatigue origin. Introducing the weakest spot concept, the fatigue origin will occur at the weakest spot. Now, if the weakest spot is not significantly weaker than the surrounding material, the actual level of weakness may have little influence on the cycles to failure and these will relate to the average strength of the specimen. This is the condition that leads to a log normal distribution.

On the other hand, if the weakest spot is significantly weaker than the associated material, it must be expected to have some influence on the cycles to failure and these will be a function of both the level of weakness of the weakest spot and the average strength of the surrounding material. Unfortunately, material imperfections do lead to weak spots that create this condition, and this results in considerable distortion of the log normal distribution and produces a distribution that can loosely be called bi-modal.

Bi-modal distributions arising from significantly weaker spots

The distribution we are interested in will arise as some combination of the normal distribution of initial strength and the distribution of the initial strength of weak spots. We require to establish the probable form of the latter distribution. For this purpose, we will assume that the occurrence and level of weakness of the weak spots are random. That is, they occur by chance. Since, being undesirable, they are subject to some form of control, the weaker the spot the less the likelihood of its occurrence.

When we examined the random occurrence of failure, we showed how they could be described by the negative exponential distribution. In the same way, this distribution can be used to describe the probability of randomly occurring levels of weakness.

We can write

$$\text{Probability of a spot being weaker than } M = 1 - e^{-aM},$$

where a is a constant.

Even if the assumption of a negative exponential distribution is not correct, the distribution of levels of weakness can clearly be expected to follow a skewed distribution approaching the same form.

Having established the forms of our two distributions, we can construct a diagram representing the situation and this is shown in Fig. 8.2. A

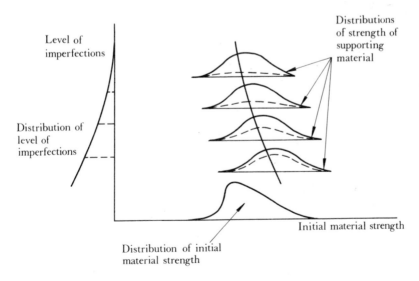

Fig. 8.2

similar form is adopted to that used to describe the fundamental strength/duty/life-to-failure relationship (Fig. 4.3).

The distribution of levels of weakness is shown on the left and a series of normal distributions describing the average strength are drawn to correspond with increments of the level of weakness.

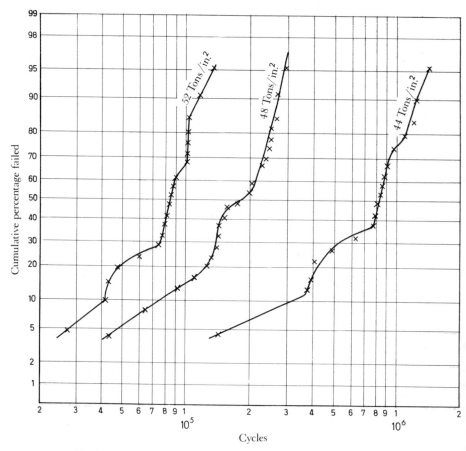

Fig. 8.3 **Cumulative probabilities of failure of a creep-resistant alloy steel at three stress levels under rotating bend tests**

The dotted distributions show the proportions exposed at various weakness levels. The normal distributions have been enclosed by curved parallel lines in the diagram, but the shape of these curves and their parallelism is assumed; they describe the relationship between the cycles to failure, level of weakness of the weak spot and average strength of the specimen.

The resulting distribution of cycles to failure has been drawn on the horizontal ordinate and can be seen to have a long tail at the low-life end. The form of the distribution of this tail will be explored more thoroughly

102

at a later stage; for the moment it will merely be stated that it does not conform with any of the usual statistical distributions. We can, however, examine it to some extent by means of an example which, as will be shown later, follows the theoretically expected form.

The example is taken from a series of rotating bend tests carried out by Howard Brook on a creep-resistant alloy steel. The results of these tests at three stress levels 52, 48, and 44 tons/in.^{2} (80, 74, and 68 hbar) are shown in Fig. 8.3 plotted on log normal paper. An excessive distortion of the log normal form at the lower end is at once apparent.

We will study the 44 tons/in.^{2} distribution. Starting at the long-life end, there are a few results that conform with the log-normal distribution—the weakest spot is not influencing the cycles to failure. Then there is a step in the distribution, which can be regarded as defining the area where a weak spot may or may not influence the cycles to failure, according to the chance of it occurring in a specimen with a high or low average strength. This may be termed an area of take-over between the parts of the distribution where the weakest spots have no influence and those where they have a major influence. The distribution then assumes a peculiar form, and there is one failure at significantly lower cycles than the remainder. This failure is where a high level of weakness of the weakest spot is combined, by chance, with a low average specimen strength. It is a point that is to be expected from a combination of the distributions shown in Fig. 8.2.

The results at 52 and 48 tons/in.^{2} will be seen to follow the same general pattern as well as can be expected within the confines of a comparatively small sample. Similar distributions resulted at other stress levels and have been omitted for clarity.

Bi-modal distributions due to a combination of short- and long-term fatigue

There is another way in which fatigue results can produce a bi-modal distribution: this occurs when the distribution of the strain range of a number of specimens embraces the kink point occurring, in the log strain-range/log cycles-to-failure curve, at the transition between short- and long-term fatigue.

The situation is depicted diagrammatically in Fig. 8.4, which is an extension of the type of diagram evolved in Fig. 4.7.

The points A and B correspond to the points on the log strain-range/log cycles-to-failure curve where the curve starts to become asymptotic with the plastic and elastic lines shown in Fig. 8.1. At these points, the slopes of the lines of degradation change due to a change in the rate of degradation.

The effect is to 'bend' the log normal distribution that we expect to obtain, and an example is shown in Fig. 8.5, plotted from data obtained by Rolls-Royce laboratories from rotating bend tests on 245 specimens

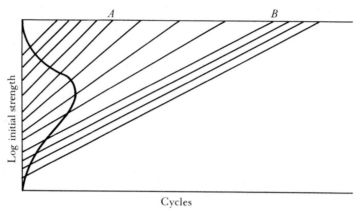

Fig. 8.4 Derivation of bi-modal distribution due to a combination of long- and short-term fatigue

cut from nimonic alloy turbine blades at cycles at constant stress at 800°C. For ease of plotting, the points have been collected into cycle bands. It will be seen that the distribution is described by two straight lines on log normal paper but that there is a constriction at the bottom end, indicating that there is a minimum cycles to failure approaching 10^5.

For another example of this case, reference is made to the work of F. Cicci, who explored the form of the distributions that arose in the area of the intersection. Among others, he has put forward the theory that the bi-modal effect is due to the spread of the strain range covering the short- and long-term regions. He carried out rotating bend tests on a maraging steel at five different stress levels, and produced bi-modal distributions of cycles to failure. A plot of his results on log normal paper is re-produced in Fig. 8.6. He also explored various distributions to describe the two parts of his overall distribution and concluded that the log normal was the best fit in both cases.

A point to note in connection with these results is the very large spread in cycles to failure that arises where both short- and long-term fatigue are present.

Minimum fatigue life

It will now be apparent to the reader that some difficulties exist in predicting the minimum fatigue life of a part, particularly if some weak spots are likely to exist. Weak spots can be caused by inclusions, damage, corrosion, notches, and physical characteristics of the material, and these are the factors that, in practice, usually dictate the minimum life of a population of parts. Where weak spots do not exist, there may well be a constriction that dictates the minimum fatigue life, but this can be established only if a large number of tests are carried out, and it can again be expected to be related to the control that is exercised over the material.

104

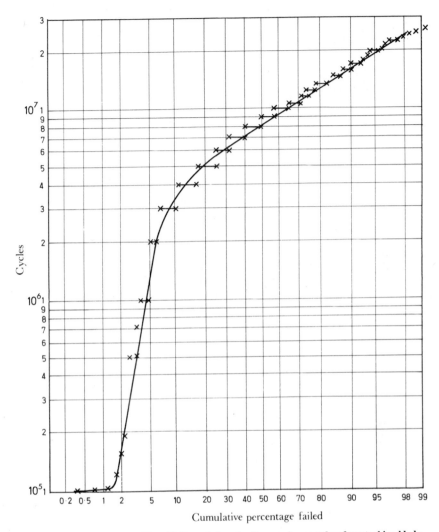

Fig. 8.5 Cumulative probability of failure of nimonic alloy specimens, taken from turbine-blade forgings under rotating bend tests

The assurance that the minimum fatigue life is acceptably high is primarily a quality problem; only in the case of material that is free from imperfections affecting the fatigue life can reasonable estimates be made from the analysis of small samples.

Tests on parts

While laboratory tests are of some interest to reliability engineers, our prime concern is with tests on actual parts or pieces cut from them, since this relates more closely to what is going to happen in practice. We will accordingly take, as our next example, a series of tests that were carried out on one inch wide strips cut from the compressor discs of an axial gas turbine. The discs used were production parts that had been rejected for inclusions, and the purpose of the tests was to establish the effect these inclusions had on the fatigue life of the discs. Three standards were tested,

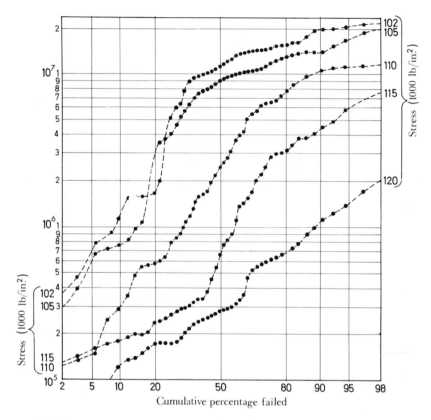

Fig. 8.6 Cumulative probability of failure of a maraging steel at five stress levels under rotating bend tests

sections containing inclusions considered unacceptable, considered acceptable, and free from inclusions. Since there was a considerable area exposed to failure, we may expect the log extreme-value distribution to apply, and the results of all the tests taken together plotted on log extreme-value paper are shown in Fig. 8.7. The fit is poor, but a re-plot on log normal paper produced a fit that was worse. The results from the sections containing no inclusions are plotted in Fig. 8.8, and show the effect of cen-

106

soring the distribution by removing the specimens that are expected to fail early. There is no reason why this distribution should fit any mathematical expression whose form could be assumed for extrapolation purposes, since it has an artificial constriction. It shows that the probability of failure is becoming remote somewhere between 4×10^5 and 5×10^5 cycles.

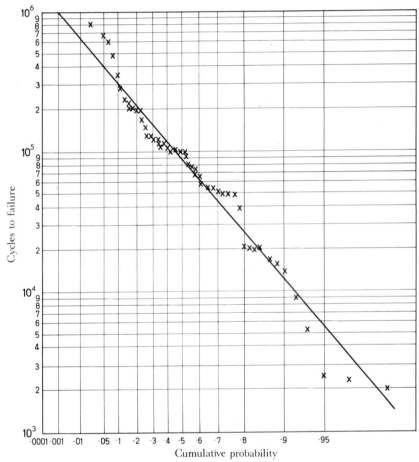

Fig. 8.7 **Tests on sections from compressor discs. Sample from total population**

Returning to the plot of the total results, the scatter is very large; the results cover a range of 400 to 1. Two explanations are offered to account for this large scatter, first the substandard nature of many of the sections tested, and second, variation in duty. The stress over the section was not uniform, due to the particular geometry, nor could its variation be defined by a statistical distribution. In the censored distribution the scatter has been reduced to more manageable proportions, a range of about 20 to 1. Over the important lower 50 per cent, the scatter is of the order of three to one. In whole discs instead of sections, this scatter could be expected to reduce further.

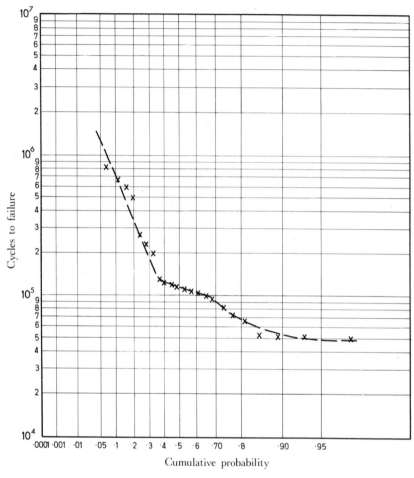

Fig. 8.8 Tests on sections from compressor discs. Samples free from magnetic indication

The effect of stress level on the scatter of cycles to failure

We can approach the question of the effect of stress level on the scatter of cycles to failure in a theoretical way, by considering Figs. 4.6 and 4.7. At different stress levels, the rate of deterioration changes (Fig. 4.6), and consequently the range of the cycles at which failures will occur (Fig. 4.7) will decrease with increase in stress. However, the scatter factors will

108

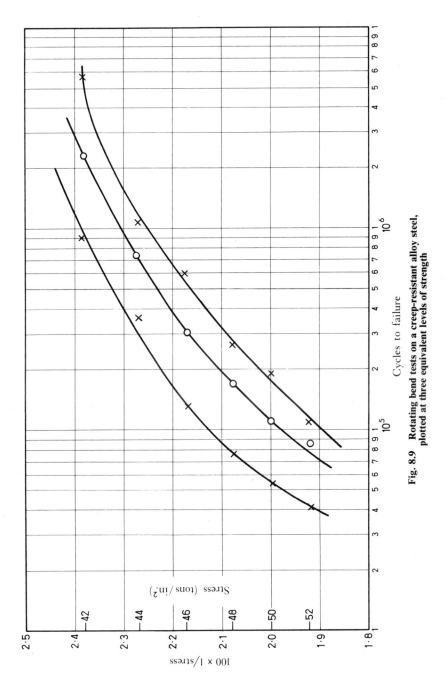

Fig. 8.9 Rotating bend tests on a creep-resistant alloy steel, plotted at three equivalent levels of strength

remain constant. If this is not apparent to the reader, he can quickly satisfy himself that it is so by using similar triangles.

If we now consider a plot of 1/stress against log cycles to failure, we can expect the failure distributions at different stress levels to fit between two parallel lines. This will be appreciated if the log scale of cycles to failure is considered in terms of its log values which are linearly spaced. Equal increments on such a scale will represent the logs of the scatter factors, which are constant.

Accordingly, in the ideal general case, if we plot two levels of strength on a 1/stress against log cycles to failure graph we expect to get two parallel lines. Given such a result, we say that there is no interaction between strength and stress with regard to cycles to failure. If the lines were not parallel we would say that there was an interaction.

We have already seen how the form of the distribution of fatigue test results can change with change of stress level, and it may be expected that this will bring about some interaction. This is often found to be the case. The spread of the failure distribution tends to increase with reduction in stress when these distributions are plotted on a log base. There is no hard and fast rule, and some investigators have found no interaction over a range of stresses, although as the stress approaches the fatigue endurance limit, it is logical that the failure distribution will increase in the upward direction.

As an example where a small amount of interaction is present, we will take Brook's results on a creep-resistant stainless steel, some of which were given in Fig. 8.3, where it was shown that the failure distributions were multi-modal. His results at six stress levels are shown in Fig. 8.9 plotted as 1/stress against log cycles to failure. The 10, 50 and 90 per cent of the distributions are shown. The lines joining these points can be taken as representing particular levels of initial strength. There is a small but inconsistent amount of interaction, until the time is reached at which the stronger material approaches its endurance limit and starts to diverge from the average material. This latter type of interaction is usually of no interest from a reliability viewpoint, our concern being with the low-strength side of the distribution.

The curve is seen to kink, and the portions on either side of the kink can both be reasonably represented by the relationship $1/D = b \log N + K$, which we have previously assumed.

9

The form of the duty distribution

It is pertinent to our general argument to examine the expected form of the duty distribution. We can look at variations in duty in three ways: variations under a constant-use condition, variation due to differences in the level of use, and the case where the duty can rise to high levels for short periods.

Variations in duty under a constant-use condition

It is reasonable to state that, if the level of use of a piece of equipment is constant, any variation in the duty to which its parts are exposed is due to variations of the parts which go to make up the equipment. For example, a number of similar engines may give the same power output, but there is some variation in temperature because of variability of thermal efficiency, the cooling system, and other causes.

A prime cause of duty variation under constant-use conditions is dimensional variability. The relationship between dimensions and duty can be anything from very simple to complex, depending on the design. The simplest case is where the load is constant, and variations in duty arise from stress variations caused by differences in the dimensions of the part or parts involved. An example is a strut subject to a direct tensile load. A more complex situation arises where a part is subject to local stress concentrations, the load on which varies due to the dimensions of associated parts.

An example where a number of dimensions contribute to the duty is illustrated in Fig. 9.1. The part A expands due to temperature, causing a bending stress in flange B which is relatively cool, resulting in a stress concentration at C. The duty at C is related to the outside diameter of A, the flange bore size and the radius at C. We have three different dimensions concerned with the actual stress that is generated.

We have previously used a dimensional variation to demonstrate the normal distribution. Most dimensions vary according to the normal distribution, a fact that makes it the prime distribution used in quality control. Accordingly, we can expect any distribution of duty that is

111

generated by dimensional variation also to follow the normal distribution.

In our example, variation in temperature also affected the duty. Such variation is likely to have a number of causes, in which case it will also be sensibly normal. Combining this with the normal distribution generated by the dimensional variation, we can expect the overall duty distribution to be normal.

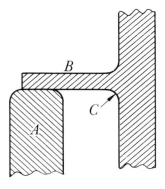

Fig. 9.1

Situations arise where the relationship between the duty and the factors that affect its level is not linear. If the variability of such factors leads to a normal distribution, the form of duty distribution will be normally distorted by the relationship between these factors and the duty.

To take a simple example, suppose that the duty is stress produced by centrifugal force and that the speed that generates this force is normally distributed. Then, since the stress is proportional to the square of the speed, the duty distribution will be normal on a base scale of x^2. It is positively skewed on linear base scale.

If the relationship is the square root instead of the square, the distribution becomes negatively skewed on a linear base scale.

Duty variation with variation in the level of use

The degree of usage that a piece of equipment is subject to will often vary considerably during its life or during an operating cycle. As an example, the usage of the parts of a motor car, say the brakes or the engine, will vary during a particular journey and between one journey and the next.

The duty that we have considered as combining with the strength to cause failure at a given time is some form of summation of a number or all the different levels of usage that the equipment is subjected to.

If we plot level of usage against time at particular levels, we shall get a distribution that cannot be expected to conform to any particular pattern. An example of such a distribution for the usage imposed on an aircraft

112

engine is shown in Fig. 9.2. The most severe condition occurring is during the aircraft take-off, but this occupies a relatively short period, and for most of the aircraft's operating life the level of usage is reasonably low.

If we plotted individual distributions for a large number of flights, we should find that both the periods at a particular condition and the level of usage at this condition were variables. Figure 9.2 shows six conditions, so we have twelve variables that can affect the overall amount of duty that the engine is subjected to. We can conveniently present the duty distribution in the form of a distribution of the continuous duty level that would have the same degrading effect as the summation of the different levels.

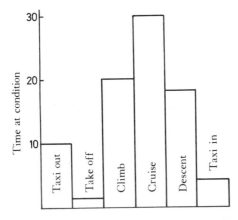

Fig. 9.2   Typical civil-aircraft flight profile

The duty × time distribution at any flight condition can be expected to be normal. Even if this is not the case, the central limit theorem will apply if we take a sample from each of these distributions and sum them: the result of such a process can be expected to be a normal distribution.

If we assume that any one level of duty has no effect on the rate of degradation at other levels of duty, we can say that the duty distribution over all the engines in use is a normal one.

If we consider particular parts of our engines, we can appreciate that the duty imposed on some of them will not follow the same pattern as that applied to the engine as a whole. A number of parts suffer primarily from thermal shock, which only occurs when the engine is opened up, and a number of others are only degraded to any extent when the level of duty is over a certain value. The highest level of stress also has an influence on fatigue life in some instances. In such cases, the duty may be related to peak rather than average values.

We will accordingly examine the type of distribution that describes the peak values. For this purpose, we will represent the duty relative to time

113

by a wave form as shown in Fig. 9.3, the distribution of peak values and instantaneous values also being shown. The latter is a normal distribution, which, as we have seen, is a reasonable assumption when the duty is related to a particular operating condition and is subject to random variation.

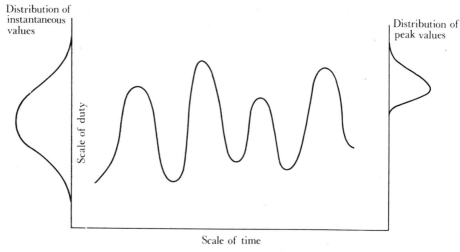

Distribution of instantaneous values

Distribution of peak values

Scale of duty

Scale of time

Fig. 9.3

Let us take the case where there is a single parameter that controls the duty level, e.g., temperature. It was shown by Rayleigh in 1880, working on sound waves, that under such conditions, the probability distribution function of the peak values is given by

$$f(h) = \frac{2h}{m^2} e^{-h^2/m^2}, \tag{9.1}$$

where h is the height of the peak and m is the root mean square of the instantaneous values. The form of this distribution of peak values is shown in Fig. 9.3, and is seen to be positively skewed.

To take a second case, suppose that we have a major low-frequency parameter that controls the duty level and that a high-frequency, low-amplitude vibration is superimposed on top of this as shown in Fig. 9.4. The distribution of the peaks closely follows the form of the instantaneous

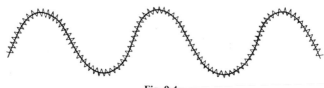

Fig. 9.4

duty distribution controlled by the major parameter which we have assumed normal.

In practice, we may expect to obtain a distribution somewhere between the two extremes, the actual form depending on the number of parameters that control the duty and the influence that they exert, that is, the extent to which the Rayleigh distribution is modified and brought nearer to the normal. The Rayleigh, normal, and a number of the intermediate distribution forms are shown in Fig. 9.5.

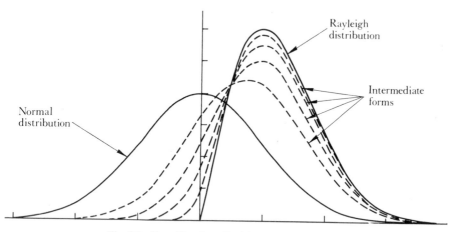

Fig. 9.5   Transition from Rayleigh to normal distribution

We will explore the Rayleigh distribution a little further. From integration of eq. (9.1), we obtain

$$F(h) = 1 - e^{-h^2/m^2}. \tag{9.2}$$

This can be transformed into

$$\log_e \frac{1}{1 - F(h)} = \frac{h^2}{m^2}. \tag{9.3}$$

So that a Rayleigh distribution appears as a straight line on log linear paper, the log scale is annotated as $1/[1 - F(t)]$, and the linear scale as h^2. The slope of the line is $1/m^2$.

The question now arises as to the effect of the distribution of peak values on the form of the duty distribution, where this represents constant levels of duty that would have the same degrading effect as the peak-value combinations that actually occur.

Two cases arise, the first where a particular peak level has no effect on the rates of degradation at other levels, in which case the duty distribution describes the sum of a large number of sample peak values and is, as before, a normal distribution.

115

In the second case, a peak level of duty above a certain value will damage the material in such a way as to promote more rapid degradation than usual at lower duty levels. Examples of this are where excessive temperature tempers the material or severe corrosive attack occurs that reduces the general resistance to corrosion.

If the peak values occurred at the beginning of a part's life, we should expect a Rayleigh distribution or a distribution approaching this form. If we assume that the peak value will occur at some random life, the normalizing influence will be increased and we shall have one of the forms of the intermediate distributions shown in Fig. 9.5.

Mention must be made of the expected duty distributions in the case of fatigue failures. A number of investigators have explored the effects of cycling specimens at different stress levels, and have formulated expressions that relate these stress levels to cycles to failure. For a small range of stress level, or where a small range of high stress combines with appreciably lower stresses, a summation of the fatigue-life usage at these levels provides a reasonable estimate of the total fatigue life, and we can expect a normal duty distribution.

This summation rule can be expressed as

$$\log_e N = N_1 a_1 + N_2 a_2 + \cdots + N_n a_n,$$

where N is the total fatigue cycles to failure,

$N_1, N_2, \ldots, N_n$ are the cycles to failure that would be experienced at stress levels maintained for proportions $a_1, a_2, \ldots, a_n$ of the total number of cycles N.

This rule can be applied to degrading mechanisms other than fatigue, such as creep.

When the range of stresses that cause fatigue failures is such that the variation in life at these stresses is of the order of say 10, the simple cumulative rule given above has been found to fail, and the rate of degradation is related to the highest stress level. In such cases, we can expect the duty distribution to have some measure of positive skew.

We can sum up this study of the duty distributions where there are differences in use level by saying that it is reasonable to expect these distributions to be sensibly normal but that exceptions arise where

(a) the duty is not directly related to a controlling parameter that is normally distributed, and

(b) the equivalent overall duty is related to the peak duty value.

Any consideration of the probable form of the duty distribution must clearly take account of the engineering considerations involved. The evidence that the author has been able to examine strongly suggests that a normal duty distribution occurs in the great majority of cases, and some of this evidence is presented in the next section. Unless the engineering suggests otherwise, the reader is recommended to assume that the duty distribution is approximately normal.

Examples that illustrate a normal duty distribution

It is not usually possible to measure a duty distribution, so direct proof of the argument for normality cannot be presented. It is, however, possible to find examples that provide some measure of substantiation, if we look

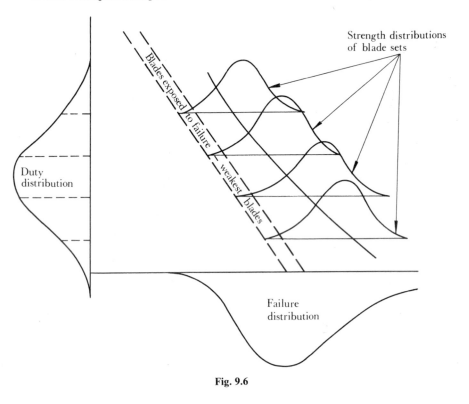

Fig. 9.6

at cases where a large number of similar components are exposed to the same duty.

When we studied the strength distribution of parts, we showed that the scatter in life to failure decreased with the area of the part exposed to failure. In the same way, if we have sets of similar parts, we can expect the weakest to fail first and the strength variation between the weakest in each set to be small. Under these circumstances, the failure distribution will be influenced to only a small extent by the strength distribution, and will tend to follow the duty distribution, particularly where the duty

117

variation is such that the duty/time-to-failure curve approximates to a straight line.

The situation is represented diagrammatically in Fig. 9.6, where $1/D$ is plotted against $\log_e t$, and the strength distribution is represented by a narrow band. The duty distribution is assumed normal and is presented as the inverse of normal on the $1/D$ scale. Since $1/x \simeq 1 - a \log_e x$ for small variations of x, the inverse of a normal distribution approximates to a log normal. The figure shows that the failure distribution follows the same form as the distribution of $1/D$, but on a log base scale. Accordingly, if the duty is normally distributed, we can expect the failure distribution to be approximately the reverse of log normal on a log scale and therefore normal on a linear scale.

Examples of where this situation occurs are the compressor and turbine blades in an axial-compressor gas-turbine engine. Mortality curves for aero-engine compressor and turbine blades which failed in airline service are shown in Fig. 9.7 plotted on normal probability paper. In both cases they indicate a normal distribution.

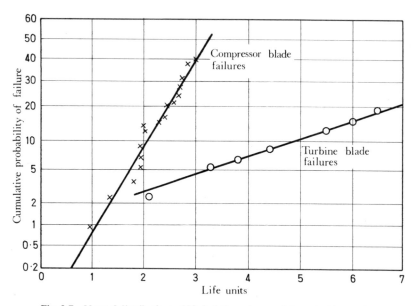

Fig. 9.7   Normal distributions of blade failures in an axial gas-turbine engine

In the case of the compressor blades, the duty distribution is the distribution of the summations of the combinations of stress levels encountered and the time during which these stress levels applied relative to each engine. Similarly, the duty distribution for the turbine blades is a summation of the combinations of temperatures and the times during which they were experienced.

118

The case when the duty can rise to high levels for short periods, or is affected by a dominant variable

The occurrence of a short period of excessive duty is normally brought about by one predominant variable, rather than the combined effect of a large number of small variables as considered in the previous case. Accordingly such occurrences cannot be described by the normal distribution. An appropriate distribution to use in such cases is the extreme-value distribution. The long skewed tail of this distribution indicates that it is of the general form that might be expected to describe such occurrences. This distribution has been found to fit variations in natural phenomena very well—for example, climatic temperature, rainfall, and wind-gust variations.

The extreme values of these natural phenomena are caused by particular circumstances or combinations of circumstances that arise by chance. Similarly, extreme levels of duty in engineering equipment are due to some special factor or combination of factors, and we can regard the extreme-value distribution as being applicable.

Another distribution that can apply is the negative exponential distribution. This distribution also describes chance occurrences satisfactorily. The distribution cannot be used to describe the whole duty distribution because, as reference to Fig. 3.1 will show, it is a single-sided distribution. It may, however, fit the important high end of the duty distribution.

Duty arising from more than one parameter

We have considered duty as a single parameter, but it is frequently the case that two or even three parameters can affect the duty—for example, stress and temperature. In the simple case, a plot can be made of the two parameters, and an example is shown in Fig. 9.8, which shows time to failure in creep of a nimonic alloy as influenced by both temperature and stress. The figure shows how changes in stress level have varying effects on time to failure, according to the temperature. There is an interaction between the two forms of duty with regard to time to failure.

The duty/time-to-failure relationship that we have discussed,

$$\frac{1}{D} = a + b \log_e t,$$

becomes confused, because of the difficulty of defining the composite value D. For the equation to hold, this becomes a complex expression relating the two parameters. In practice, one of the parameters is usually dominant, and the duty distribution is closely allied to the one describing this parameter. If this is not the case, the effect of any interaction is present in the distribution. In Fig. 9.8, temperature is seen to be the dominant parameter.

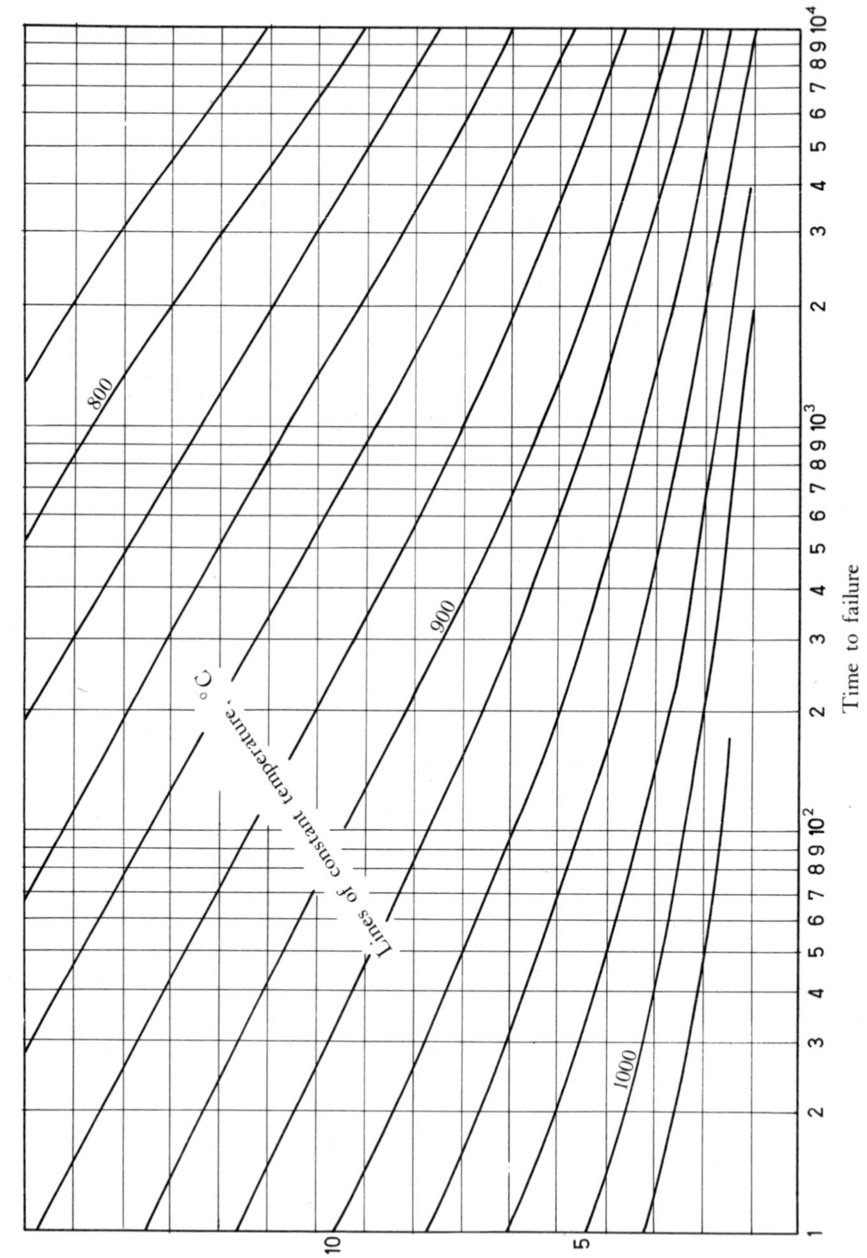

Fig. 9.8 Plot of creep life to failure of a nimonic alloy; an example of the combined effect on life of a two-parameter duty

120

10

The case where both strength and duty are variables

We are now in a position to study the form of the distributions that arise when both the strength and duty are variables. This is the situation that invariably arises when equipment is in customer use, and also applies to some test programmes.

With the assumption that we have a duty/time-to-failure relationship of the form $1/D = b \log_e t + h$ (eq. (4.1)), we can represent the situation diagrammatically in the manner shown in Fig. 10.1. If the strength and duty distributions are known, together with the duty/time-to-failure relationship, it would appear possible to derive the time-to-failure distribution. To do this mathematically would be extremely difficult, if not impossible, since there is no reason to suppose that all the resulting time-to-failure distributions follow a form that can be described by general mathematical expressions.

The simplest method open to us, and the one used by the author, is known as the Monte Carlo method, which consists of taking a large number of random selections and putting the results into an ordered form. In

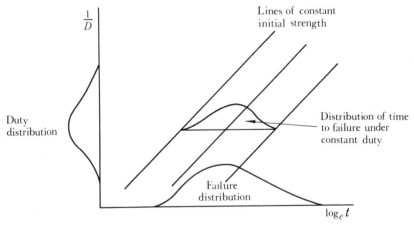

Fig. 10.1 Diagrammatic representation of the case where duty and strength are variables

simple terms, it involves taking a large number of dips into bags containing all the possible combinations, and seeing what is drawn out.

In the case of our particular problem, a first dip is made into a bag containing a large number of values that together are described by the duty distribution. The value that comes out defines a level of duty, and taking the time-to-failure distribution appropriate to this level, a second dip is made into a bag containing lifetime values described by this distribution. The lifetime value that comes out of the bag is the time to failure that occurs with the particular chance selection. If the process is repeated a large number of times, the times to failure that result are described by the failure distribution.

The process would be tedious if done manually, but it can be done quickly by a computer, and this has enabled the author to study the forms of the time-to-failure distributions that can be expected to arise from various combinations of forms and spreads of strength and duty distributions.

We will examine the results obtained from a series of analyses of the ideal theoretical case, where a normal duty distribution is combined with log normal distributions of times to failure at specific duty levels, the latter arising from a normal initial-strength distribution.

For a part with a large area exposed to failure, the log extreme-value distribution might be preferable to the log normal, but the latter is convenient to use and describes the case where a small area is exposed to failure. There is not enough difference between the two distributions to have a significant effect on the result, provided the variation in strength is small.

Given that the forms of the strength and duty distributions are defined, the factors that have a bearing on the time-to-failure distribution are:

(a) The spread of the duty distribution
(b) The spread of the strength distribution
(c) The duty/time-to-failure relationship
(d) Any interaction that exists between duty and strength with regard to time to failure.

Taking factor (d), Fig. 10.1 shows no interaction between duty and strength, the lines of constant strength being parallel. This is the condition commonly encountered in the case of fatigue, though it cannot be regarded as universally true. For the purposes of our analysis, we will assume that no interaction is present.

Analyses were made varying the spread of the duty and strength distributions and also the duty/time-to-failure relationship in turn, the other two factors being held constant. Some of the results of this exercise, together with the relevant conditions, are shown in Figs. 10.2, 10.3, and 10.4, which enables a comparison to be made of the effects of variability in the particular circumstances.

122

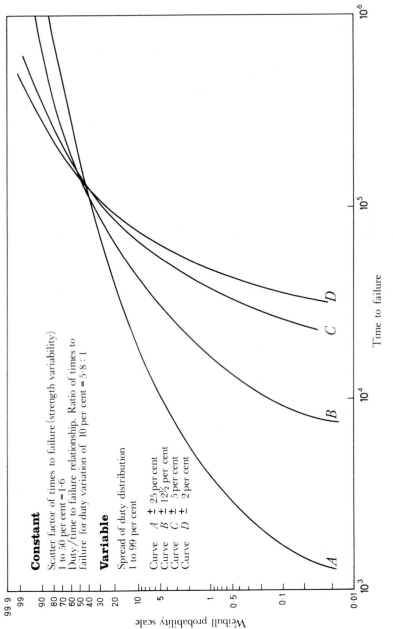

Constant

Scatter factor of times to failure (strength variability)
1 to 50 per cent = 1·6
Duty/time to failure relationship. Ratio of times to
failure for duty variation of 10 per cent = 5·8 : 1

Variable

Spread of duty distribution
1 to 99 per cent

Curve *A* ± 25 per cent
Curve *B* ± 12½ per cent
Curve *C* ± 5 per cent
Curve *D* ± 2 per cent

Weibull probability scale

Time to failure

Fig. 10.2 General case—effect of duty variation

123

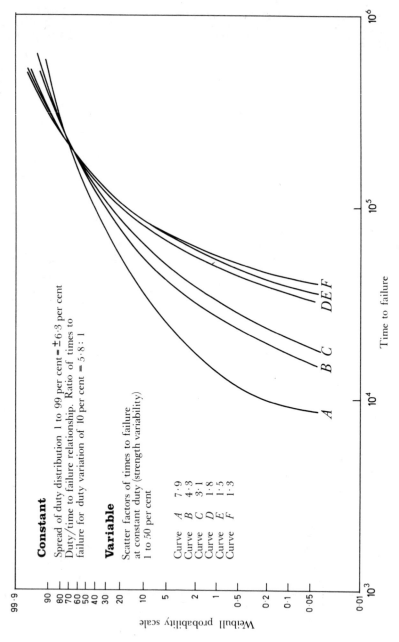

Constant

Spread of duty distribution 1 to 99 per cent = $\pm 6\cdot3$ per cent
Duty/time to failure relationship. Ratio of times to failure for duty variation of 10 per cent = $5\cdot8:1$

Variable

Scatter factors of times to failure at constant duty (strength variability) 1 to 50 per cent

Curve A	$7\cdot9$
Curve B	$4\cdot3$
Curve C	$3\cdot1$
Curve D	$1\cdot8$
Curve E	$1\cdot5$
Curve F	$1\cdot3$

Weibull probability scale

Time to failure

Fig. 10.3   General case—effect of strength variation

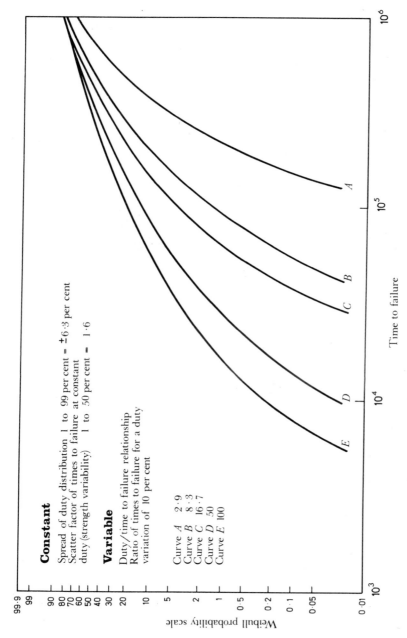

Constant

Spread of duty distribution 1 to 99 per cent = ±6·3 per cent
Scatter factor of times to failure at constant
duty (strength variability)   1 to 50 per cent = 1·6

Variable

Duty/time to failure relationship
Ratio of times to failure for a duty
variation of 10 per cent

Curve A   2·9
Curve B   8·3
Curve C   16·7
Curve D   50
Curve E   100

Weibull probability scale

Time to failure

Fig. 10.4   General case—effect of variation in duty/time-to-failure relationship

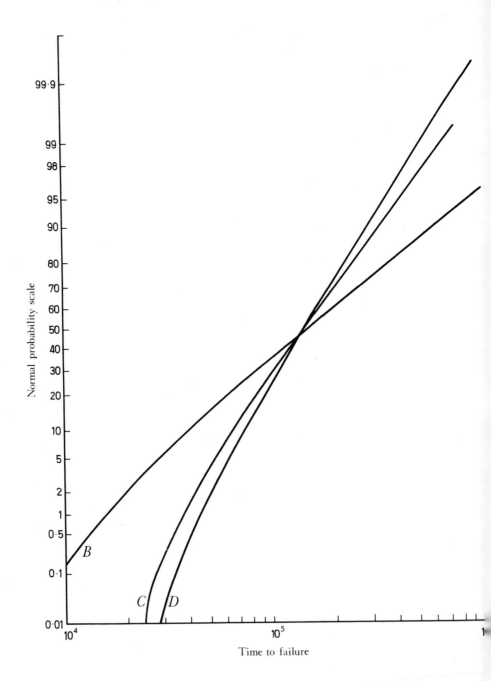

Fig. 10.5 Approach of the time-to-failure distribution to log normal
with reduction in duty variability

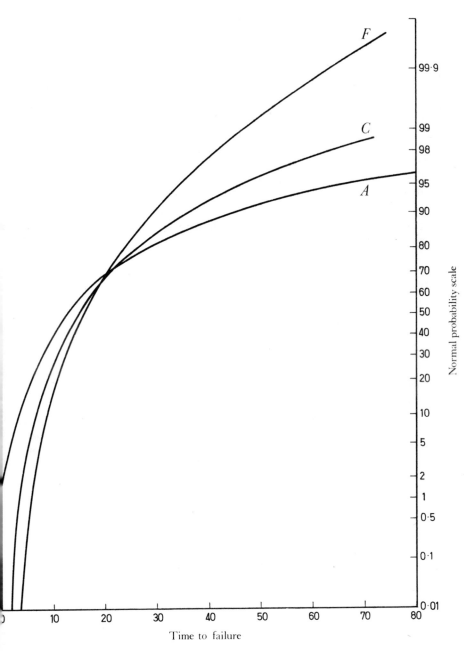

Fig. 10.6   Approach of the time-to-failure distribution to normal
with reduction in strength variability

127

The curves themselves do not conform to a Weibull form, the slopes being too small at the lower probabilities and too large at the higher to enable them to be adjusted to the straight line that must be obtained before the curve can be described by the Weibull function. In most cases, a portion in the centre can be fitted to the Weibull function.

As the duty variable decreases, the resulting time-to-failure distribution can be expected to become representative of that describing the time to failure at constant duty, and to approach the log normal form. This effect is illustrated in Fig. 10.5, which is a re-plot of the curves shown in Fig. 10.2 on log normal paper. Similarly as the variability in initial dynamic strength reduces, the life-to-failure distribution will tend towards the normal and this is shown in Fig. 10.6, which is a re-plot on normal paper of the curves shown in Fig. 10.3. The values of the parameters selected for the example show a case where the resulting distributions conform to a log normal better than the normal. This is the case most frequently met with in practice but as the following actual examples will show the tendency can be towards either normal or log normal.

Distributions of time to failure experienced in practice

Examples of the distributions of time to failure taken from service experience with Rolls Royce engines will now be examined.

Example 1. A case of gear teeth failures due to fatigue. In Fig. 10.7, the failure data is shown plotted in three ways: on Weibull, normal, and log normal probability papers. The curve on the Weibull paper cannot be satisfactorily adjusted to conform with a straight line, so that it does not represent a Weibull form. It does, however, exactly match curve *E* of Fig. 10.4, which was derived theoretically for the general case where there was a major change in time to failure with small changes in duty. This situation can be expected in this instance. The example illustrates the general case.

It is instructive to examine the plots on normal and log normal paper. That on normal paper is a pronounced curve, probably indicative of variation in time to failure at a constant duty level, while the log normal plot is a straight line, so the duty can be considered as having a small amount of variation.

These conclusions, coupled with the large variation in life to failure shown by the data, indicate a duty/time-to-failure relationship with a small slope, such as arises at the long-life end of a stress/cycles-to-failure fatigue curve as depicted in Fig. 10.8. The data plots are as would be expected from engineering considerations.

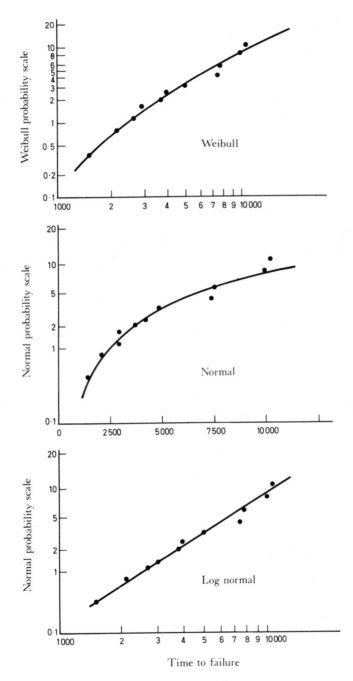

Fig. 10.7   Gear-teeth failures

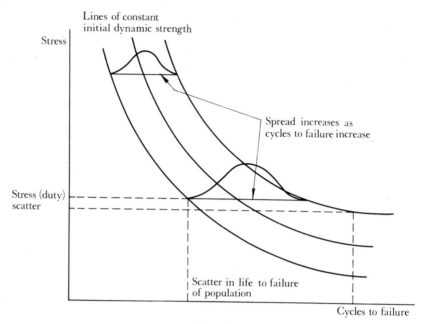

Fig. 10.8

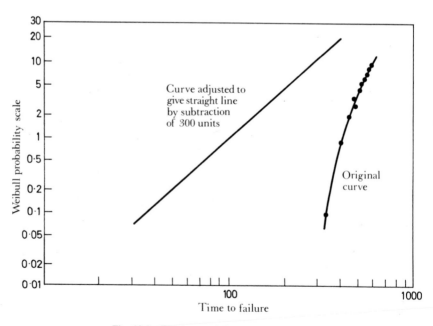

Fig. 10.9　Bearing track failures due to fatigue

Example 2. A case of ball bearing track failure due to rolling contact fatigue.
The data from this example is shown plotted on Weibull probability paper
in Fig. 10.9. The curve can be adjusted to produce a straight line, showing
that the distribution is of a Weibull form.

Bearing failures, whether on test or in service, frequently conform to a
Weibull distribution, and the example is included to show that the Weibull
is applicable in some cases.

Example 3. A case of ball bearing separator failure due to fatigue. This
example is similar to the example of gear-tooth failures. The data is shown
plotted on Weibull, normal and log normal paper in Fig. 10.10. The curve
on Weibull paper is sensibly a straight line with a tendency to curvature
at the top. That on normal paper is a definite curve, but the plot on log
normal paper shows a good fit to the log normal distributions. It can be
concluded that the situation illustrated in Fig. 10.8 is again applicable.

It may be noted that while a straight-line plot on Weibull paper usually
indicates that there is a probability of failure at zero life, such a conclusion
is untenable in this instance, because, the failure mechanism being fatigue,
there must be a period of deterioration prior to the first failure.

The effect of skew duty distributions

In the cases in Examples 1 and 3, where the form of the life to failure
distribution is dominated by that of the strength distribution, any modest
amount of skew that the duty distribution has will have an insignificant
effect on the life-to-failure distribution. On the other hand, where the
strength variation is small, skewness of the duty distribution becomes
important and it is relevant to consider its effect.

The general effect is illustrated in Fig. 10.11. This shows a normal distribution associated with a typical Weibull plot as shown in Figs. 10.2 to
10.4; the way that this curve becomes distorted when the distribution is
skewed in either direction can be seen.

It will be observed that the sense of the duty scale is reversed, high duty
being on the left and low duty on the right. If the duty distribution has its
long tail towards the high-duty end the effect is to straighten out the curve,
whereas if it is skewed in the other direction, the curvature is increased,
bringing it closer to the Weibull form.

Constant and falling failure rates associated with time-dependent failures. The case of ball and roller bearings

As a duty/time-to-failure relationship approaches the condition where the
curve becomes asymptotic with the time axis, the range of possible times
to failure clearly becomes large. Any duty variation that is present

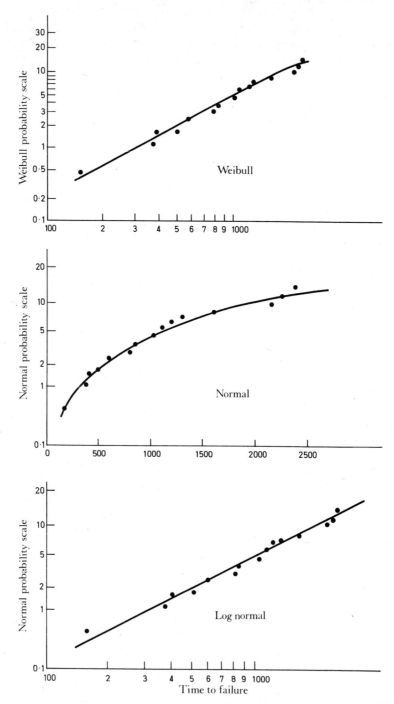

Fig. 10.10   Ball-bearing separator failures

increases this range, and the effect is to produce a constant or falling failure rate with time.

This can be seen by reference to Fig. 10.4. Any curve of Weibull form that had a similar range of time to failure as curve A in this figure will, when adjusted to a straight line, clearly have a β value of less than 1.

It is accordingly quite possible for failures to occur because of a time-dependent mechanism without showing an increasing failure rate with time. This case often arises with ball and roller bearing failures, which satisfy the conditions necessary to produce this result.

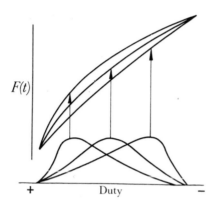

Fig. 10.11   Effect of skewed distribution on the form of the time-to-failure distribution

When a number of bearings are tested under the same conditions and the same load, there are considerable differences in the duty, that is in the stress actually imposed on the tracks and balls. Such differences arise due to variations in the area and form of the contact between the balls and tracks which are dependent both on dimension variation and the hardness of the parts. Another variable is the manner in which the balls rotate, which affects the uniformity of duty experienced by points on the ball surface.

As an example of the effect of the differences in duty generated by differences that can occur within a bearing, reference is made to the work of Zaretsky, Parker, Anderson, and Reichard at the Lewis Research Centre, Cleveland, Ohio. They explored the effect of differences in hardness between the balls and inner track on the life of deep grooved ball bearings. Table 10.1 is reproduced from their results and illustrates that an optimum difference in hardness of 2 on the Rockwell C scale gives the greatest life.

The large differences between the lives at which 10 per cent failures occurred will be noted. While not included in the table, their report shows that the scatter factor between 10 per cent and 50 per cent associated with the optimum condition was about 3.

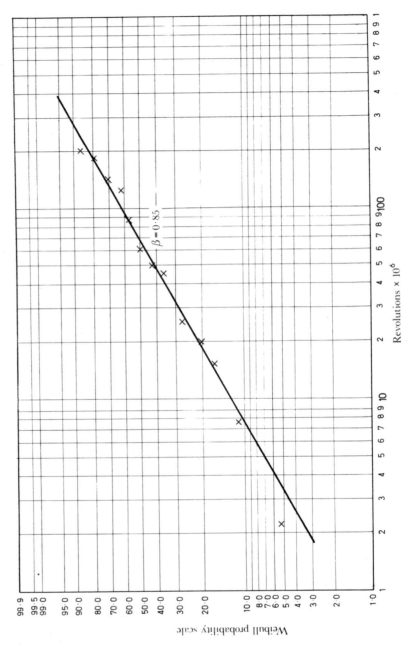

Fig. 10.12   Ball-bearing test results showing decreasing failure rate with lifetime

134

Table 10.1

Nominal ball Rockwell C hardness	Nominal H (difference in hardness between balls and race)	10 per cent fatigue life (millions of inner race revolutions)	Failure index (number of bearings failed out of number of bearings tested)
60	−3	21	14 out of 28
63	0	77	11 out of 25
65	2	106	12 out of 28
66	3	74	14 out of 27

(*Courtesy* Lewis Research Centre)

Many Weibull plots of bearing tests produce β values of about 1. An example of a plot of ball failures occurring during a series of bearing tests is shown in Fig. 10.12, and in this case $\beta = 0.85$, but $\beta = 1$ means that the failure rate after a period α is constant.

It is interesting to compare these results with the plot of bearing failures shown in Fig. 10.9, which has a β-value of 2·2. The reason for this high β-value can be found from a consideration of the mode of failure. The bearings in question were seriously overloaded during part of the operating cycle, so that the slope of the duty/time-to-failure curve was relatively steep and the overall range of times to failure too small to produce a constant failure rate.

11

The effect of 'weak spots'

So far our considerations of the situation have been confined to cases of strength distribution of material that, while exhibiting variability, has no dominant characteristic that causes its distribution to depart appreciably from normality. Unfortunately, in our imperfect world, material is not always perfect, nor are the fabrication processes to which it is subjected. The level of strength of a piece of material can be considerably reduced by the introduction of a 'weak spot'. These weak spots may take various forms such as inclusions of a foreign material, voids, processing or physical irregularities. While some may be classed as quality defects, they may not all be detectable by known control processes.

The effect of a weak spot on time to failure is related to the following factors.

(a) The size and intensity of the weak spot.
(b) The relationship between the size and intensity of the weak spot, its location, and the strength of the material.
(c) The strength of the supporting material.

In some cases the strength of the supporting material is a negligible factor; for example, in the breakdown of insulation, the fact that the surrounding material continues to insulate is unimportant. On the other hand the effect of a crack is dependent on the resistance to crack propagation of the material surrounding it.

In general, weak spots can be expected to occur at random, and the probability of a given level of weakness to decrease as the level increases. This probability could be described in some cases by the negative exponential distribution, in other cases the double exponential might be applicable.

These considerations can give rise to a whole family of strength distributions, but a theoretical examination of two examples is sufficient to indicate the general pattern that they can be expected to follow.

In the first example, it is assumed that the strength at the weak spot is not influenced by the strength of the supporting material. Sixty-five per cent of the population have weak spots the probable size or intensity of

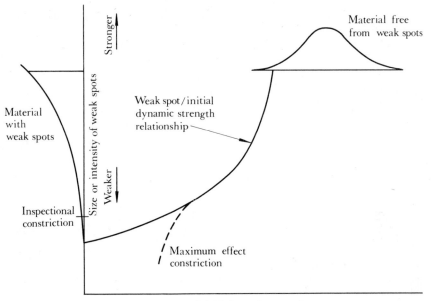

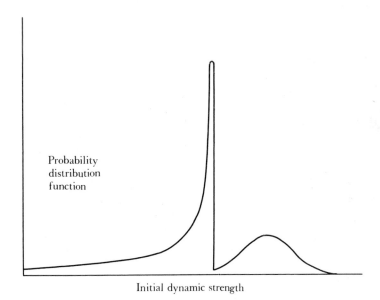

Fig. 11.1 'Weak spot' case, supporting material having no influence

which is described by the negative exponential distribution, the initial strength of the remainder following a normal probability distribution. An exponential relationship is assumed between size or intensity of the weak spots and the initial strength.

The situation is set out in diagrammatic form in Fig. 11.1, which also shows the P.D.F. of the initial strength, which can be generated from the diagram. In practice, it is usually found that there is a constriction present that truncates the distribution at the low-lifetime end and leads to a low-lifetime limit. Such a constriction can arise in two ways; first, weak spots above a certain size may induce a level of weakness of such a magnitude that it is not increased by the introduction of even larger weak spots.

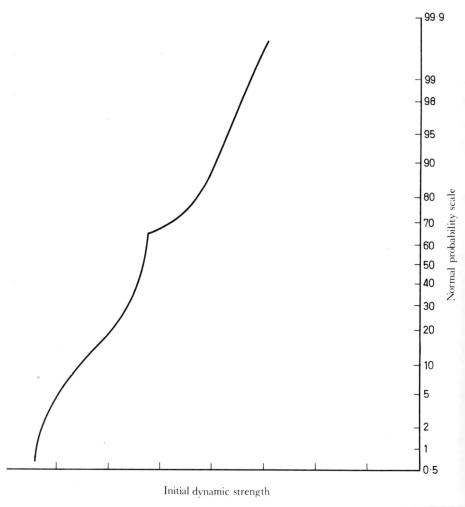

Initial dynamic strength

Fig. 11.2   Cumulative probability function (derived from Fig. 11.1)

Fatigue tests carried out with artificially introduced inclusions have indicated that this is the case. When this condition exists, the curve representing the weak spot/strength relationship has the S-shaped form shown dotted in the figure.

The second type of constriction is where manufacturing or inspectional constraints impose an upper limit on the amount of weakness. This effect is shown in the diagram by the line truncating the distribution of the size or intensity of the weak spot.

Returning to the form of initial strength distribution that the example

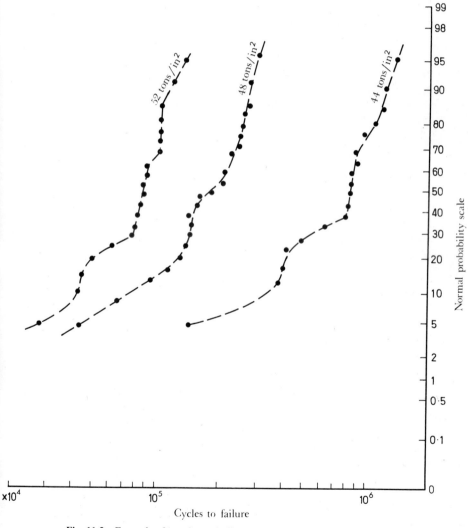

Fig. 11.3   Example of 'weak spot' effect. Fatigue test on a stainless steel

generates, it will be seen that there is peak probability associated with large numbers of comparatively small weak spots. The cumulative probability is shown on normal probability paper in Fig. 11.2. The distribution has been drawn assuming a 'weak spot' constriction as shown in the previous figure and its effect can be observed at the lower end of the scale.

The distribution shown in Fig. 11.2 can be regarded as being typical of the weak spot condition, where only a proportion of the population contain weak spots. It will now be compared with an example of time-to-failure distribution at constant duty levels, which produces the same form but which, since it shows the probability of time to failure instead of initial strength, must be shown on a log base scale.

Example 1. Fatigue tests on a stainless steel. This example relates to data obtained from a series of fatigue tests on a stainless steel at stress levels of 52, 48, and 44 tons/in.[2] (80, 74, and 68 hbar) and which is shown plotted on log normal probability paper in Fig. 11.3. It may be noted that all the test pieces were from the same cast of material. The area where the weak spots start to influence the distributions can be observed, as can the point where the weak spots become the prime strength criteria.

It is relevant to consider the effect that the area of the part that is exposed to failure has on the form of the distribution. The larger this area, the greater the likelihood of weak spots being present, so that the distribution describing the probable size and intensity of these becomes modified and embraces a larger proportion of the population, until when weak spots are present in the whole population, the upper portion of the distributions shown in the examples disappear. The distribution of initial strength of the proportion of the population free from weak spots may tend towards the double exponential type. These changes do not alter the characteristic form of the distribution.

The effect of duty variations

The effect of variations in duty in the weak spot case is difficult to estimate, because of the difference that must exist between the duty/life-to-failure relationship of weak spots and material free from weak spots. In practice, duty variability seems to make little difference to the general form of the distribution, although the spread is increased and some smoothing occurs. The following example illustrates this.

Example 1. Tests on bearing materials. The data is plotted on Weibull paper in Fig. 11.4 and relates to tests that were carried out to compare different materials with regard to their suitability for use for bearing tracks. Discs of the different materials were loaded onto a number of balls and

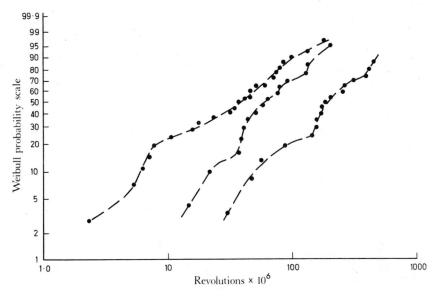

Fig. 11.4 Tests on bearing materials

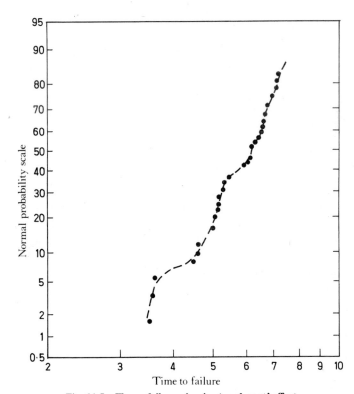

Fig. 11.5 Flange failures showing 'weak spot' effect

141

rotated until the surface broke up in rolling-contact fatigue. As stated previously some variability in the stress applied to the material must be expected since this is affected by varying hardness and ball variations. The curves are seen to be characteristic of the weak-spot type.

Example 2. A case of flange failures in fatigue due to high bending stresses. The plot on Weibull paper is shown in Fig. 11.5. The curve follows the characteristic weak-spot form, and there is evidence of a constraint limiting the spread at the low-lifetime end of the distribution.

Example 3. A case of compressor-blade failure and Example 4. A case of planet-gear failure. Both examples are shown plotted in Fig. 11.6. The number of failures is small in both cases, but both curves have a strong indication of being of the weak-spot type.

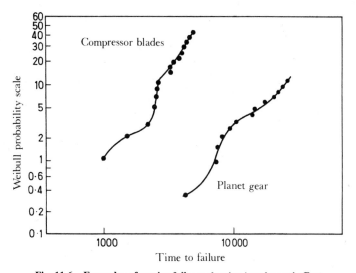

Fig. 11.6   Examples of service failures showing 'weak spot' effect

The weak-spot type of distribution that has been discussed should not be confused with those that arise due to random quality faults which eliminate themselves as life proceeds with the result that the failure rate decreases with time. The situation is shown in the early life portion of the well-known bathtub curve. An example of such a case relative to bearing failures is shown in Fig. 12.1 in the next chapter. The failures in weak-spot cases are not random relative to life and the failure rate is generally increasing with time or cycles.

12

Mixed distributions

We have examined forms of distribution that were not describable by mathematical expressions and in some cases were rather complex. These distributions were however generally capable of being split up into parts each of which could be described by a mathematical expression. They were *mixed* distributions. If a distribution is composed of two or more different distributions it is termed *bi-modal*, *tri-modal*, and so on.

In this chapter we will consider causes of mixed distributions, other than those already discussed, and for simplicity we will confine our study to bi-modal ones. We will also look at ways in which they can be handled.

The causes of bi-modal distributions

Bi-modal distributions describing part failures can arise in three ways.

(a) There is a bi-modal strength distribution.
(b) There is a bi-modal duty distribution.
(c) The distribution describes two modes of failure.

We will look at these causes in turn.

Bi-modal strength distributions   If, instead of parts manufactured from material containing weak spots of varying intensity, we have the situation where a few parts out of a population have some defect or weakness which is not present in the remainder of the population and that causes them to fail prematurely, the resulting life-to-failure distribution has a different characteristic form.

In the case of quality faults, we may have a few isolated instances of poor quality that have been allowed to slip through, or be faced with a whole batch of defective parts. The isolated instances are likely to reveal themselves as random early failures, and clearly, since they eliminate themselves by failing, they may be expected to produce a falling local failure rate. We have the situation illustrated by the bathtub curve or two portions of this curve. An example of such a curve relating to bearing failures is given in Fig. 12.1: the lower portion only relates to three failures and the line cannot be determined with any degree of certainty, although the line drawn actually passes through the three points. It has a Weibull slope of 0·7, indicating a falling local failure rate with time symptomatic of quality faults. It will be seen that the subsequent points fall on a straight line, which would not have been the case if the early failures had not occurred.

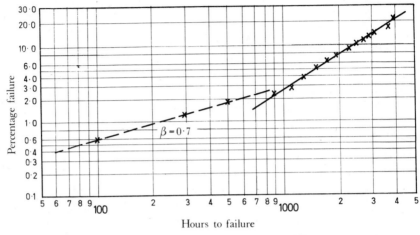

Fig. 12.1   Bi-modal distribution of bearing failures

If we assume that all failures after the first three were due to old age, then the probability of old age failures, as plotted, has been influenced by the early 'quality' failures. If the latter are omitted from the calculation, the old-age failures would plot as a curve.

It is worth making the point that when a part is not seriously sub-standard, and this part fails, it is equivalent to carrying out an accelerated test and that it may be seen as a warning that parts to the specified standard are liable to fail at rather longer life. Such a warning can be valuable and it may be unwise to put a failure down to poor quality and only take quality-control action. The question 'How poor?' should also be asked.

Bi-modal duty distributions   If we draw a distribution covering the duty imposed on a motor-car suspension when some of the cars involved nor-mally travel over rough mountain tracks and the remainder main roads, we expect a bi-modal duty distribution. While this particular example is obvious, the fact that different conditions or different users lead to different duty distributions may not always be obvious, and some bi-modal effect may be present when it is not expected.

An example of a bi-modal failure distribution due to a bi-modal duty effect is shown on Weibull paper in Fig. 12.2. This example relates to the failures in creep of aero-engine turbine blades. The creep strength of these blades falls off very rapidly with increase in temperature, and the earlier

144

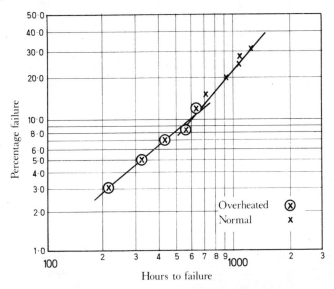

Fig. 12.2 Bi-modal distribution of turbine-blade failures

failures shown were all found to be associated with excessively high temperatures when examined after failure. The later failures were, as far as could be determined, old-age failures following normal usage. The failures associated with overheating are indicated in the figure. Since there are two types of duty, excessive and normal, it is sensible to analyse the two separately, and the result is shown in Fig. 12.3.

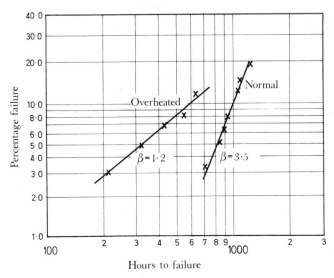

Fig. 12.3 Breakdown of bi-modal distribution of turbine-blade failures

The high temperatures experienced by the early failures can be assumed to be a random effect and also subject to a good deal of variation. The duty distribution will accordingly have a large spread. This is confirmed by the slope of the Weibull line describing the early failures, $\beta = 1\cdot2$. It can also be seen that $\gamma = 0$ for this line, indicating that overheating failures could occur at any lifetime. In reality, the curve would probably be found to become asymptotic at some low life if sufficient data were available.

The normal failures have been isolated from the overheat failures for analytical purposes. As long as we know which are which, this presents no problems. Where both types of failure are liable to occur together and they cannot be differentiated, we must use the method described in the next section.

Bi-modal distributions which describe two modes of failure Where two different modes of failure apply to the same part and the mode applicable to specific failures cannot be determined by subsequent examination, we must adopt an approach that enables us to estimate the proportion of the total failures due to each cause.

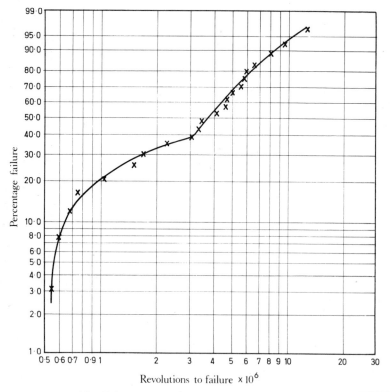

Fig. 12.4 Bearing failures with bi-modal distribution

A good instance of where such an approach can be required is the case of ball bearing failures. By the time these failures are discovered and investigated, the damage is often too extensive for the cause to be ascertained with any certainty. We may be able to trace one cause and take action on the assumption that all the failures were due to it, only to find that failures continue because there were two causes and we have dealt with only one.

A Weibull plot of bearing failures due to two causes is shown in Fig. 12.4. We can see at a glance that it is bi-modal, and provided we have no reason to suspect a bi-modal duty distribution, we conclude that we have two modes of failure, one of which may be associated with some low strength or poor-quality parts. Alternatively, one may be ball failures and the other track failures. At any rate we can appreciate that we have two problems to deal with.

To analyse the two distributions, the first step must be to separate them. We make the assumption that the early failures are the result of a mode that will continue to occur, irrespective of the life of the bearing. Where the early failures show a decreasing local failure rate, $\beta < 1$, as will be shown to be the case in the example, we may question this assumption and feel that they are due to quality defects that will eliminate themselves, but for the purpose of exploring the technique, we will continue on the basis that the assumption is true. The technique we use is illustrated

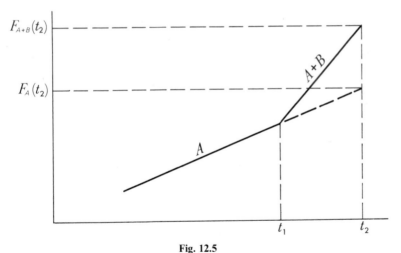

Fig. 12.5

diagrammatically in Fig. 12.5, where the two failure modes are designated A and B. At time T we can read off $F_A(T)$ and $F_{A-B}(T)$, and thus calculate $F_B(T)$. In the same way, we obtain other values of F_B, and are able to plot the distribution of failure B. The distribution of failure A requires no adjustment. The analysis of the bi-modal distribution shown in Fig. 12.5 is set out in Fig. 12.6.

147

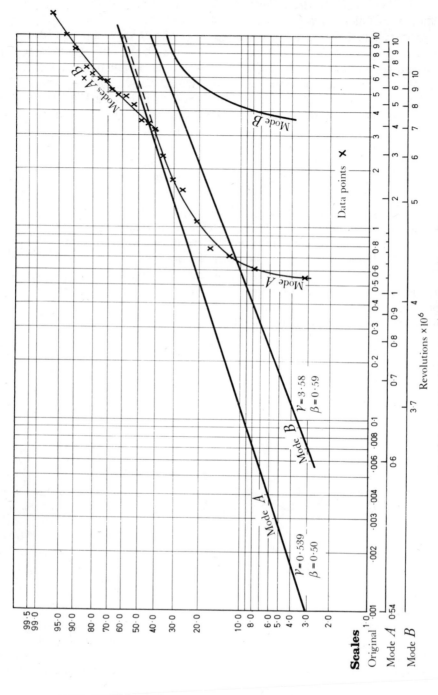

Fig. 12.6 Analysis of bi-modal distribution of bearing failures

148

The two failure modes have been termed A and B as in Fig. 12.6. The first step is to straighten out the portion of the distribution that represents mode A. For the curve representing the early failures, γ is found to be 0·539, and subtracting this value produces the straight line marked 'mode A' in the figure. Working back from this line, the original curve is extrapolated by adding γ, and this is shown dashed in the figure. Subtracting this extrapolated curve from the portion of the original curve that corresponds to the two failure modes being present produces a curve representing mode B. The final step is to straighten out this curve so that it can be extrapolated; using $\gamma = 3·58$, we obtain the straight line marked mode B.

It will have become clear to the reader that some judgement is necessary when analysing bi-modal distributions. For each particular case, the decision must be taken as whether the two portions of the distribution are likely to occur concurrently or not, and the method of analysis must be adjusted accordingly.

13

Degradation and replacement curves

So far we have been examining the characteristics of failures. Let us now turn to parts that do not reach the stage of failure because they are either replaced or salvaged during maintenance inspection. These parts are clearly not as reliable as we would wish, and the actual inspection of them costs money quite apart from any replacement cost. If we could draw the equivalent of a mortality curve showing the proportion of parts that have reached a given stage of deterioration at any given life, we should be able, not only to plan for their most economical use, but to predict the number of replacements required and the cost of the components in terms of cost per hour. This is clearly a most important curve. We call such a curve a *degradation* curve to distinguish it from the mortality curve which relates to actual failure.

The arguments that we have pursued relative to the form of a mortality curve apply equally well to a degradation curve. We are simply considering a condition where the strength has degraded to a constant level rather less than the level that results in failure.

The construction of degradation curves

When we draw mortality curves, we know the lives at which the failures occurred and are able to plot points corresponding to these lives. With a degradation curve we do not know these lives. When we carry out maintenance inspection we discover that a proportion of the components have cracked, or otherwise degraded, and this occurred at some unknown life subsequent to the previous inspection. We must modify the methods we used to construct mortality curves to take account of this. We will develop the method by means of a series of examples.

Starting with a simple case, we will suppose that maintenance inspection is carried out at regular intervals on all the components in use, and call the times at which this is done $t_1, t_2, t_3, \ldots, t_n$. Suppose that at t_1 we reject a proportion q_1. This represents the cumulative percentage that has degraded to a rejectable degree up to this time. Thus, q_1 is the same as $F(t_1)$, and is the first point on our degradation curve. At t_2 we reject q_2, which represents the proportion of those inspected that reach a rejectable standard during the period $t_2 - t_1$. By the product rule, we see that $F(t_2) = 1 - (1 - q_1)(1 - q_2)$. At t_3 we reject q_3, and $F(t_3) = 1 - (1 - q_3) \times (1 - F(t_2))$. Clearly, we are following the same procedure as was used to draw mortality curves using proportion methods.

The real-life situation rarely fits the simple case that has been described. In practice it is more usual to find that the times at which maintenance inspection is carried out vary considerably. This variation may be due to extension of the period between maintenance, or be caused by the equipment being taken out of service for some reason and the opportunity being taken to do the maintenance inspection.

Under such circumstances it becomes necessary to utilize lifetime bands so as to obtain a reasonable sample size from which the proportion rejected can be estimated. These bands need not cover equal periods of time, but it is important that the number of components inspected in each band should be sufficient. It is desirable that at least 5 degraded components should be recorded in each band, as with less than this the accuracy falls off rapidly.

The actual components inspected in any lifetime band will not necessarily have been inspected in the band immediately preceding it. This means that we can no longer accumulate the proportion rejected using the product of the proportion surviving in each band. We should be taking account of the same components at the time they were potential rejections, but were not actually inspected, and also when they were rejected. As a result, the curve would estimate a higher proportion of rejections than really occurred.

For our next example we will suppose that some components were inspected at t_1 and all the remainder at t_2, at both times a proportion being rejected. At t_3 a sample was inspected, this sample being chosen without reference to whether the first inspection was at t_1 or t_2.

As before, we can write

$$F(t_1) = q_1, \qquad F(t_2) = q_2.$$

At t_3, the chance of a component being rejected is dependent on whether it was previously inspected at t_1 or t_2. Let $q_{3,1}$ be the proportion of those components rejected at t_3 which had been previously inspected at t_1, and $q_{3,2}$ those previously inspected at t_2. We can now write

$$F(t_3) = 1 - (1 - q_{3,1})(1 - F(t_1))$$

or

$$F(t_3) = 1 - (1 - q_{3,2})(1 - F(t_2)).$$

The accuracy of our estimations of $F(t_3)$ is dependent on the number of rejects from which the values of $q_{3,1}$ and $q_{3,2}$ are calculated. If the number of rejects is sufficiently large in each case, it is a sound procedure to average the resulting $F(t_3)$'s, but if either value is liable to error, due to being derived from a small sample, the average will be liable to bias. This bias will be carried forward if the $F(t)$-values are used to calculate $F(t)$ for subsequent lifetime bands.

We will examine two alternative ways of proceeding which will minimize the effect of any bias and have the virtue of simplicity.

The first of these procedures is to plot all the values of $F(t)$ that we calculate, preferably on probability paper, and put the best-fitting curve through the points taking cognizance of any points that may be in error due to small sample sizes. The $F(t)$-values used to calculate subsequent points are estimated from the curve. It is appreciated that this procedure is unlikely to appeal to statisticians, but it should be acceptable to engineers, and it provides a good estimate of the curve.

The second method is to consider the overall proportion rejected in any lifetime band, instead of taking the proportion relative to the time of previous inspection.

We then write the general expression

$$F(t_n) = 1 - (1 - q_n)\left(1 - \begin{array}{c}\text{proportion of sample expected to have}\\\text{been rejected at earlier inspection}\end{array}\right),$$

(13.1)

q_n being the proportion rejected out of all components inspected in lifetime band t_n.

We see that this method has the advantage that the sample size from which values of q are calculated has been increased, and additionally some simplification has been obtained.

Taking the last term in the general equation (13.1), we can interpret this as meaning the average probability that components are omitted from the sample because they were rejected previously.

In the case of our last sample, we now write

$$F(t_3) = 1 - (1 - q_3)\left(\frac{N_1(1 - F(t_1)) + N_2(1 - F(t_2))}{N_1 + N_2}\right),$$

where N_1 and N_2 are the numbers inspected at $F(t_3)$ previously inspected at t_1 and t_2.

And our general equation (13.1) now becomes

$$F(t_n) = 1 - (1 - q_n)\left(\frac{N_0 + N_1(1 - F(t_1)) + \cdots + N_{n-1}(1 - F(t_n - 1))}{N_n}\right)$$

(13.2)

where $n > 2$, and N_0 is the number inspected for the first time at t_0.

The calculations involved when using this method can conveniently be

Table 13.1 Calculation of degradation curve, method 1

Lifetime band	Total inspected	Previous inspections		Total rejected	Proportion rejected	F(t)
		Number	Lifetime band			
0–2000	—	—	—	0	0	0
2000–2500	2769	—	—	7	0·003	0·003
2500–3000	1562	71	2000–2500	9	0·006	$1 - (1 - 0{\cdot}006)\left[\dfrac{1562 - 71 + 71(1 - 0{\cdot}003)}{1562}\right] = 0{\cdot}006$
3000–3500	1349	0	2000–2500	16	0·012	$1 - (1 - 0{\cdot}012)\left[\dfrac{1349 - 142 + 142(1 - 0{\cdot}006)}{1349}\right] = 0{\cdot}012$
		142	2500–3000			
3500–4000	1562	71	2000–2500	25	0·016	$1 - (1 - 0{\cdot}016)\left[\dfrac{1562 - 142 + 71(1 - 0{\cdot}009)}{1562}\right] = 0{\cdot}016$
		71	2500–3000			
		0	3000–3500			
		142				

Table 13.1 (continued)

Lifetime band	Total inspected	Previous inspections — Number	Previous inspections — Lifetime band	Total rejected	Proportion rejected	$F(t)$
4000–4500	2201	710	2000–2500	44	0·020	$1 - (1 - 0\text{·}020)\dfrac{\begin{array}{c}2201 - 1136 + 710(1 - 0\text{·}003) + 213(1 - 0\text{·}006)\\ + 71(1 - 0\text{·}012) + 142(1 - 0\text{·}016)\end{array}}{2201} = 0\text{·}023$
		213	2500–3000			
		71	3000–3500			
		142	3500–4000			
		1136				
4500–5000	781	355	2000–2500	23	0·029	$1 - (1 - 0\text{·}029)\dfrac{\begin{array}{c}355(1 - 0\text{·}003) + 142(1 - 0\text{·}006)\\ + 213(1 - 0\text{·}012) + 71(1 - 0\text{·}016)\end{array}}{781} = 0\text{·}036$
		142	2500–3000			
		213	3000–3500			
		71	3500–4000			
		0	4000–4500			
		781				

tabulated, as is done in Table 13.1. The data used relates to the onset of cracking on jet-engine turbine blades due to thermal shock. The resulting curve is shown on Weibull probability paper in Fig. 13.1.

The methods of calculating the degradation curve we have studied are all dependent on knowing the maintenance inspection times of all the pieces of equipment involved. This amount of data may not always be available, but we usually know the period between maintenance inspections. If we use this average period instead of the actual period for each part, the calculation is greatly simplified, although with some loss of accuracy. Provided the rate at which parts reach the rejection standard is reasonably constant, this loss of accuracy will be negligible for practical purposes. Only when the rate increases rapidly with time will the resulting curve be a serious underestimate of the truth.

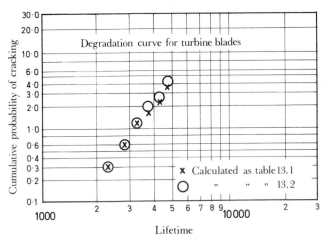

Fig. 13.1 Degradation curve for turbine blades

Referring to the method described previously, we approximate the estimate of $F(t_n)$ by writing

$$F(t_n) = 1 - (1 - q_n)\left(1 - \begin{array}{l}\text{proportion of the sample expected to} \\ \text{have been rejected up to and including} \\ t_{n-1}, \text{ where } t_n - t_{n-1} \text{ is the average} \\ \text{time between maintenance inspections}\end{array}\right)$$

To make the calculation as simple as possible, it is advisable to select lifetime band widths that divide directly into the average period between maintenance inspections; the last term in the equation will then be the same as an appropriate value of $F(t)$ already calculated for a previous band. Until the average period between maintenance inspections is greater than the time since the earliest rejections, the points on the curve are the actual proportion rejected in each lifetime band with no correction applied.

155

An example of the tabulation required to calculate degradation curves using this simplified method is set out in Table 13.2. The same data regarding the onset of cracking, as was employed in the last example, is used. The points calculated by this method are plotted in Fig. 13.1 for comparison with the more exact method.

When failures occur which could have been prevented if earlier maintenance inspection had been carried out, these should be included with the rejections when calculating the curves.

Table 13.2

Lifetime band	Total inspected	Rejected	Proportion rejected	Average inspection period	$F(t)$	Result given by previous method
Up to 2000	—	0	0	1500	0	0
2000–2500	2769	7	0·003	1500	0·003	0·003
2500–3000	1562	9	0·006	1500	0·006	0·006
3000–3500	1349	16	0·012	1500	0·012	0·012
3500–4000	1562	25	0·016	1500	$1 - (1 - 0·016)(1 - 0·003) = 0·019$	0·016
4000–4500	2201	44	0·020	1500	$1 - (1 - 0·020)(1 - 0·006) = 0·025$	0·023
4500–5000	781	23	0·029	1500	$1 - (1 - 0·029)(1 - 0·012) = 0·041$	0·036

Practical use of degradation curves

There are two categories to be considered in practice: those where maintenance action can restore the component to the as-new condition, and those where this is not possible. An example of the former is a wooden boat hull, where scraping off the old varnish, rubbing down, and revarnishing restores the boat hull to the virgin condition. An example of the latter is a car body, where removing the rust and repainting does not restore to the new condition, but merely slows down the degradation for a temporary period before the rate of rusting returns to its pre-maintenance rate.

The apparent failure rate for the case where maintenance is effective is related to the maintenance interval (Fig. 13.2). The apparent reliability can be doubled by halving the maintenance interval, quadrupled by quartering the maintenance interval, and so on. More complex interrelationships apply where the failure rate versus time characteristic is non linear.

An analysis of available practical data should be made to try to establish the correlation between failure rate and component life. From this data, a

156

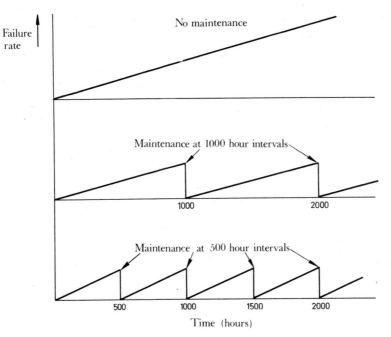

Fig. 13.2

rational decision can be made about the frequency of maintenance required to produce an acceptable level of reliability. Where safety considerations do not apply, this decision can be made on a straightforward economic basis to minimize the operating costs, taking into account the costs of failures and the costs of maintenance (Fig. 13.3).

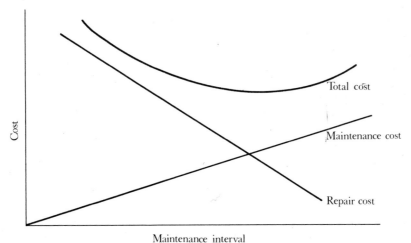

Fig. 13.3

The potential for saving money using these types of analysis can be very considerable where maintenance costs are high and the costs of failure are high, or the consequences of failures unacceptable. But it all depends on being able to produce a realistic degradation curve.

Conversely, where the degradation curve can be established and shows that the failure rate does not increase with time, then maintenance can be reduced to a minimum, as it is in no way contributing to improved reliability.

The concepts of maintainability and the effects of maintenance are discussed further in chapter 15.

14

The χ^2-distribution, tests for frequency, confidence limits for M.T.B.F.

We have seen that the Poisson distribution gave us a means of determining the probability of a specified number of events, given that we know the number we expected to occur on average. We now come to a distribution that does the same thing and gives a similar result, but has a wider field of application and in some cases is more convenient to use.

This distribution is the chi-squared distribution, denoted by χ^2 and pronounced kigh to rhyme with high. It is defined by

$$\chi^2 = \sum \left[\frac{(n_o - n_e)^2}{n_e} \right], \tag{14.1}$$

where n_o is the number observed, and n_e is the number expected.

χ^2 is accordingly a function of the way in which the number of observed events varies from the number expected.

The $\sum$ sign shows that the value of χ^2 takes account of all probabilities associated with an occurrence, so that it can be used where an event can have a number of outcomes.

It will be seen that the value of χ^2 must always be positive, and this is the reason for using the notation χ^2 rather than χ. χ^2 should be regarded as a single symbol.

There is a definable probability of the actual number of events that occur having a specific difference from the number expected, and consequently there is a given probability associated with a particular value of χ^2. We can represent this by a probability distribution with values of χ^2 as the base scale. This, then, is the χ^2 distribution.

We have defined χ^2 as relating to all outcomes of an event, and the larger the number of possible outcomes, the greater the value of χ^2 expected. We accordingly associate χ^2-values with the number of ways in which the frequency of an occurrence can vary, and call these *degrees of freedom*. For example, when we take a sample of one we get a fixed value, and there are no degrees of freedom. By taking a second sample of one, we introduce one way in which our result can vary, and we have one degree of freedom.

Each time we take one additional sample, the number of degrees of freedom increases by one, so that the number of degrees of freedom, when we take n samples, is $n - 1$.

Where we are concerned with a particular value of χ^2, we must indicate both the probability and the number of degrees of freedom that are associated with this value. We write these as subscripts. The general form is $\chi^2_{v,\alpha}$, where α is the probability and v the number of degrees of freedom, for example $\chi^2_{(6,0.95)}$ means χ^2 with a 95 per cent probability and 6 degrees of freedom. Tables of χ^2-values are given in all books of statistical tables.

Actual χ^2-distributions for 1 and 6 degrees of freedom are illustrated in Fig. 14.1. It will be observed that the distribution is skewed with a small number of degrees of freedom. As the number of degrees of freedom are increased, the χ^2-distribution becomes closer to the normal distribution, until finally it coincides with it.

Having established what the χ^2-distribution is, we will now look at the ways in which it can be used by engineers concerned with reliability.

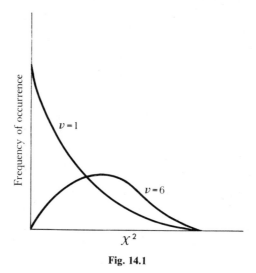

Fig. 14.1

Comparing frequencies

As is our custom, we will develop the method by means of examples. We will suppose that similar items have been delivered to two different customers A and B. Customer A has received 108 of these items and has had 22 failures, customer B has received 72 and had 8 failures. The question arises as to whether there is any significant difference in use between customers A and B.

160

To use χ^2, we must first estimate what we expect, and we do this by combining the results from A and B and say that out of 180 items we expect 30 failures. We can then say that we expect failures as follows.

$$\text{Customer } A, \quad \frac{108 \times 30}{180} = 18$$

$$\text{Customer } B, \quad \frac{72 \times 30}{180} = 12$$

We now introduce a correction called Yates' continuity correction, which is performed simply by the subtraction of 0·5 from the $(n_o - n_e)$-value before squaring. (We will examine the reason for this correction shortly.)

Continuing our example,

$$\text{For customer } A, \quad \chi^2 = \frac{(|22 - 18| - \frac{1}{2})^2}{18} = 0\cdot680$$

$$\text{For customer } B, \quad \chi^2 = \frac{(|8 - 12| - \frac{1}{2})^2}{12} = 1\cdot021$$

$$\chi^2 = \overline{1\cdot701}$$

The number of degrees of freedom is 1, since we have one way in which the frequency can vary, i.e., given customer A, customer B can be different, and vice versa.

We now consult the χ^2-table, and find that for one degree of freedom the value at 80 per cent probability is 1·642, and at 90 per cent is 2·706. There is accordingly just over an 80 per cent probability or $\frac{1}{5}$ chance that the customers are different. The case is not proven, but it may be thought worth while to do some further investigation.

When doing a χ^2-test for frequency, it is convenient to tabulate the calculation and the above example can be set out as in Table 14.1.

Table 14.1

Customer	Exposed	n_o	n_e	$\lvert n_o - n_e \rvert - \frac{1}{2}$	$(\lvert n_o - n_e \rvert - \frac{1}{2})^2/n_e$
A	108	22	18	3·5	0·680
B	72	8	12	3·5	1·021
Total	180	30	30		$1\cdot701 = \chi^2$

It is necessary to restrict the use of this test to cases where the expected number is at least 5. Where it is less, the small denominator gives inflated values of χ^2 and hence incorrect results.

Yates' continuity correction We have seen that the χ^2-distribution is a continuous one, so that there is a value of χ^2 corresponding to any fractional number of failures. In our example, the number of failures must be a whole number and the resulting distribution of χ^2 is accordingly a histogram.

We accordingly make a correction that adjusts for the use of a continuous distribution, although we are actually dealing with a stepped one. This correction is done by subtracting 0·5 from the difference between the observed and expected values, and we write

$$\chi^2 = \frac{(|n_o - n_e| - 0\cdot5)^2}{n_e}.$$

The vertical lines indicate that the value of $n_o - n_e$ is always treated as positive whatever the sign is.

It may be noted that this correction tends to overcorrect, except in cases where the probabilities of the two outcomes of each event are equal.

Confidence limits for M.T.B.F.

Subject to certain constrictions, the probability of χ^2 can be equated to the cumulative Poisson probability that a number of events n will not be exceeded, so that a relationship exists between χ^2 and n. This relationship is actually

$$\chi^2_{2n,\,\alpha} = 2n, \tag{14.2}$$

where n is a whole number.

We can use this equation to evaluate confidence limits for M.T.B.F.'s in the constant-failure-rate case, if we substitute T/m for n, where T is the total time of operation and m the M.T.B.F. Then,

$$\chi^2_{2n,\,\alpha} = \frac{2T}{m}, \qquad m = \frac{2T}{\chi^2_{2n,\,\alpha}}. \tag{14.3}$$

By setting the level of confidence α that we require, we can calculate the confidence limits as follows.

Upper confidence limit for m (single sided) $= m_u = \dfrac{2T}{\chi^2_{(2n,\,1-\alpha)}}$

$$\tag{14.4}$$

Lower confidence limit for m (single sided) $= m_l = \dfrac{2T}{\chi^2_{(2n+2,\,\alpha)}}.$

$$\tag{14.5}$$

For double-sided limits $\alpha/2$ would be substituted for α. Note that for the lower confidence limit, $2n + 2$ degrees of freedom are used instead of

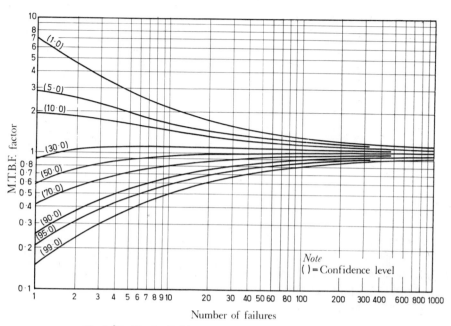

Fig. 14.2 Single-sided lower confidence limit M.T.B.F. factors
(based on number of failures and confidence level shown)

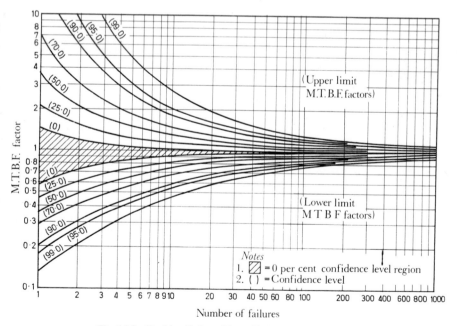

Fig. 14.3 Double-sided confidence limit M.T.B.F. factors
(based on number of failures and confidence level shown)

$2n$. It has been shown by Epstein that this is required when the data relates to a period of time that is independent of the number of failures; when the time of exposure terminates at a definite number of failures, then $2n$ degrees of freedom should be used.

Thomas A. Simonds has provided us with a quick way of calculating these confidence limits. The nominal value of $m = T/n$ and dividing eqs. (14.4) and (14.5) by this equation gives us

$$\frac{m_u}{m} = \frac{2n}{\chi^2_{(2n, 1-\alpha)}}, \tag{14.6}$$

$$\frac{m_l}{m} = \frac{2n}{\chi^2_{(2n+2, \alpha)}}. \tag{14.7}$$

Simonds calls m_u/m and m_l/m multiplication factors, and has produced charts which give these factors for different numbers of failures and different confidence levels. These charts for single-sided and double-sided confidence levels are given in Figs. 14.2 and 14.3. To use the chart, the multiplication factor on the left-hand ordinate is read off relative to the number of failures that have occurred and the level of confidence required. The calculated M.T.B.F. is then multiplied by the factor to give the M.T.B.F. with the degree of confidence.

15

Simple systems, multiple items, and the effect of maintenance on their reliability

The reliability of simple systems

In this chapter we will start by considering the reliability of simple systems where there is some measure of redundancy present.

During the conceptual or design stage of a complex product, such as an aircraft, questions arise on the need for redundancy and on the configuration of the component parts of a system that will provide the best reliability in the most economical way. These questions can only be answered where the reliabilities of the various components are known, and in this chapter we will assume that it has been possible to estimate these.

Given a simple system for which an overall reliability estimate is required, the first step must be to consider the need for a reliability block diagram. A reliability block diagram is one that illustrates the reliability dependence of the various components that go to make up a system—it is not necessarily the same as a functional diagram.

When there is no redundancy, and the operation of the system is dependent on the successful functioning of all its component parts, the reliability block diagram is simply a number of blocks in series as shown in Fig. 15.1(a), in which A, B, C, D, E, and F represent the components. The reliability of the system $R_S = R_A R_B R_C R_D R_E R_F$, by the product rule.

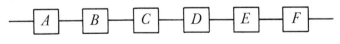

Fig. 15.1

There is clearly little purpose in drawing reliability block diagrams for simple series systems, or for the active redundancy case with two components in parallel. For all other cases, it is recommended that the diagram should be drawn.

We will develop the methods by means of examples. For the first example,

165

we will take a system which comprises a pump connected by a pipe to a control valve, the purpose of which is to maintain a constant upstream pressure.

The possible failure modes and their probabilities of failure over the period we are concerned with are as follows.

Loss of pump output	Probability of failure, a
Leakage associated with the pipe or connections	Probability of failure, b
Control unit provides too low a pressure	Probability of failure, c

Leakage is regarded as always constituting failure of the system but, provided there is a redundant system, failure to maintain pressure by one pump-control unit combination would not constitute a failure, as one such combination would be capable of maintaining the required pressure.

Two alternative configurations are suggested:

Configuration 1. Simple series system, whose reliability block diagram is shown in Fig. 15.2.

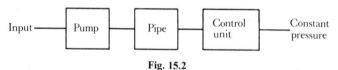

Fig. 15.2

Configuration 2. Duplicate system giving active redundancy, whose reliability block diagram is shown in Fig. 15.3.

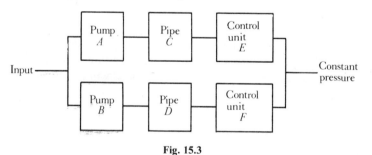

Fig. 15.3

We will consider these configurations in turn. ·

Configuration 1. Here, we have a simple series system, so we use the product rule and write

$$R_{\text{system}} = (1 - a)(1 - b)(1 - c)$$
$$= 1 - (a + b + c - ab - ac - bc + abc).$$

166

We could also have used the addition law and, noting that the three modes of failure are all mutually exclusive, written down the same answer.

Configuration 2. This can be solved by either the addition law or the product and redundancy rules. We will do it both ways as examples. First, we use the addition law.

We proceed by writing down in Table 15.1 all the events and combinations of events that could occur accompanied by failure. Against each event, we put the probability of its occurrence, and also the number of ways in which failure could occur.

Table 15.1

Event	Probability	Number of failure combinations
1. Both pumps fail	a^2	1
2. Both units fail	c^2	1
3. Pump A and unit E fail	ac	1
4. Pump B and unit F fail	ac	1
5. Both units and both pumps fail	a^2c^2	1
6. Both pumps and unit E fail	a^2c	2
7. Both pumps and unit F fail	a^2c	2
8. Both units and pump A fail	ac^2	2
9. Both units and pump B fail	ac^2	2
10. Pipe C fails	b	1
11. Pipe D fails	b	1
12. Both pipes fail	b^2	2
13–21. Events 1 to 9 combined with event 10		One more than for events 1 to 9
22–30. Events 1 to 9 combined with event 11		One more than for events 1 to 9
31–39. Events 1 to 9 combined with event 12		Two more than for events 1 to 9

The number of failure combinations is one where, for example, both pumps fail, since there is only one way in which the failure can take place. Where both pumps and units fail, there are seven more combinations, giving nine in all:

> Both pumps fail
> Both units fail
> Pump A and unit E fail
> Pump B and unit F fail
> Both pumps and unit E fail
> Both pumps and unit F fail
> Both units and pump A fail
> Both units and pump B fail
> Both pumps and both units fail.

167

We are now in a position to write down the reliability of the system using the addition law. The last column provides us with the sign of the terms in the expression. Where the number is odd we put a plus sign and where it is even a minus sign; the reason for this can be understood by reference to Fig. 15.3.

We can write

$$R = 1 - (a^2 + c^2 + 2ac + a^2c^2 - 2ac^2 - 2a^2c + 2b - b^2 - 2a^2b$$
$$- 2bc^2 - 4abc - 2a^2bc^2 + 4abc^2 + 4a^2bc + a^2b^2 + b^2c^2$$
$$+ 2ab^2c + a^2b^2c^2 - 2ab^2c^2 - 2a^2b^2c).$$

The reader will have become aware that this process involves a degree of care if the right answer is to be obtained. This particular problem can be tackled more easily by the product and redundancy rules:

$$R_{\text{pump}+\text{unit}} = 1 - (a + c - ac)$$

$$R_{\text{pipe}} = 1 - b$$

$$R_{\text{parallel pumps and units}} = 1 - (a + c - ac)^2.$$

There being redundancy we multiply the unreliabilities for the pumps and units, but for the pipes we multiply the reliabilities because the second pipe gives rise to less reliability, not more.

$$R_{\text{two pipes}} = (1 - b)^2$$

$$R_{\text{system}} = (1 - (a + c - ac)^2)(1 - b)^2$$

When multiplied out, this is the same as the answer we obtained using the addition rule. The two methods provide a very convenient means of checking results.

We will now take a second example, and suppose that the failure of the pipe and its connections has been eliminated by re-design, but that the control unit has a failure mode that allows the output pressure to increase and that such a failure constitutes a failure of the system. The two types of control-unit failure cannot occur together, so that q and r for one unit become mutually exclusive.

We will use the nomenclature of Table 15.2.

Table 15.2

Event	Probability of occurrence
Loss of pump output	p
Control unit provides too low a pressure	q
Control unit provides too high a pressure	r

Again, two systems are suggested as alternatives (Fig. 15.4), and we consider each configuration in turn.

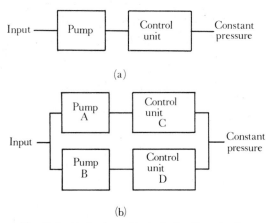

(a)

(b)

Fig. 15.4 (a) Configuration 1. (b) Configuration 2

Configuration 1. Simple series system. We tabulate the results as in Table 15.3, and use the addition law to obtain

$$R = 1 - (p + q + r - pq - pr).$$

Table 15.3

Event	Probability	Number of failure combinations
1. Pump fails	p	1
2. Unit fails low pressure	q	1
3. Unit fails high pressure	r	1
4. Pump fails and unit fails low pressure	pq	2
5. Pump fails and unit fails high pressure	pr	2

This example could also have been solved with the aid of a simple diagram, as shown in Fig. 15.5, which gives the possible combinations.

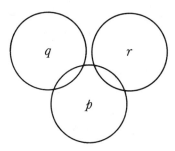

Fig. 15.5

The problem can also be done by the product rule, but here there is a pitfall for the unwary. The reliability of the system is dependent on the reliabilities of the pump and control unit, the two blocks in the diagram. We must work out the reliability of each block and then multiply the results together:

$$R_{control\ unit} = 1 - q - r$$
$$R_{system} = (1 - p)(1 - q - r)$$
$$= 1 - (p + q + r - pq - pr),$$

which is the result we obtained previously.

Configuration 2. Duplicate system with active redundancy. We compile Table 15.4 and then, using the addition law, obtain

$$R = 1 - (p^2 + q^2 + 2pq - 2p^2q - 2pq^2 + p^2q^2 + 2r - r^2 - 2p^2r + p^2r^2).$$

The reliability of this configuration cannot be calculated using the product rule, as this necessitates finding an expression for the reliability of the control unit, which cannot be done as one failure is redundant and the other not.

Table 15.4

Event	Probability	Number of failure configurations
1. Both pumps fail	p^2	1
2. Both control units fail low pressure	q^2	1
3. Pump A and control unit D low pressure	pq	1
4. Pump B and control unit C low pressure	pq	1
5. Both pumps and unit C low pressure	p^2q	2
6. Both pumps and unit D low pressure	p^2q	2
7. Both units low pressure and pump A	pq^2	2
8. Both units low pressure and pump B	pq^2	2
9. Both pumps and both control units low pressure	p^2q^2	9
10. Unit C fails high pressure	r	1
11. Unit D fails high pressure	r	1
12. Both units fail high pressure	r^2	2
13. Both pumps unit C high pressure	p^2r	2
14. Both pumps unit D high pressure	p^2r	2
15. Both pumps both units high pressure	p^2r^2	3

Stand-by redundancy We will now take the case of stand-by redundancy. For our example we will use a system similar to the second configuration in the last example, except that a switch is introduced that automatically switches the flow through the redundant pump-control unit combination if the first combination fails. We will assume that neither pump nor control

170

unit are exposed to failure when they are not in operation. The reliability block diagram is shown in Fig. 15.6.

An advantage of this system is that if the first control unit allows too high a pressure to occur, the system does not fail. The disadvantage is that we introduce the unreliability of the switch, which we will suppose can fail in two ways:

Fail to switch when it should with probability u
Switch when it should not with probability w.

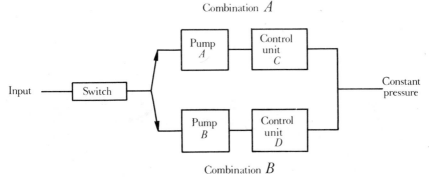

Fig. 15.6

From our previous studies, we can write the probability of failure for a single pump-control unit combination as

$$P = p + q + r - pq - pr,$$

and since the probabilities of the two combinations may be different, we will designate these P_A and P_B. We will assume that the failure rate represented by the probabilities is constant over the time being considered.

We will examine the probability of both configurations failing. If combination A is taken as that operating at the start, it may fail at any time and B will be required to take over. Let the time of failure of combination A be t. Then,

Probability of both combinations failing $= \displaystyle\int_0^1 P_A P_B (1 - t)\, dt = \frac{P_A P_B}{2}.$

We can now proceed with our analysis of the system, and we do this by considering all the events that can happen to one switch and the events causing failure associated with each one (Table 15.5). None of the events connected with the switch can occur together, so we can write the reliability of the system as

$$R_{\text{system}} = 1 - \left[(1 - u - w)\left(\frac{P_A P_B}{2}\right) + uP_A + wP_B \right].$$

171

Table 15.5

Event	Probability of failure
Switch functions correctly	$(1 - u - w)$
Both combinations fail	$P_A P_B/2$
Switch fails to work when it should	u
Combination A fails	P_A
Switch works when it should not	w
Combination B fails	P_B

In these examples, we have used symbols denoting the probability of a particular failure during a particular period. We can, if we wish, substitute the expressions for unreliability, for example $1 - e^{-\lambda t}$, where the local failure rate is constant, or $\exp\{-[(t - \gamma)/\eta]^\beta\}$ if the Weibull distribution is appropriate.

When a system contains a redundant element, the period with which we are concerned is normally fairly short. In the case of aircraft systems, it will be the period of a flight or that between routine inspections. During such a period, the failure rate of a particular mode of failure is likely to remain substantially constant even if it varies over the whole life of the component it applies to. As we have seen, the assumption of a constant local failure rate yields a simple solution to the stand-by redundancy case.

Where we wish to relate the reliability of a system to life and the system contains some time-related failure modes, the simple procedure is to assume constant failure rates over life increments and calculate the reliability for each increment. We can then calculate the mortality curve for the system in the normal way.

The reliability of multiple items

Where a piece of equipment is composed of a number of different items, or where a single item has more than one failure mode, we shall often want to combine the reliabilities of the various items or modes of failure in order to work out the overall reliability of the equipment.

We will approach the probabilities of the failure or survival of a number of items by considering the laws of chance, and these can be quite easily appreciated if we use dice and playing cards as examples.

The laws of chance For our first study, we will use dice, and it will be readily appreciated that since a die has six numbered sides and provided it is a good die, we shall have an equal chance of getting any number between one and six each time we throw.

Suppose we want to know the chance of getting a particular number, say a one both times in consecutive throws. The chance of getting a one on the first throw is $\frac{1}{6}$, so before we start the second throw we shall have abandoned all hope of two ones five times out of six and the sixth time we shall have thrown a one and still be in the running. The chance of getting a one on the second throw is also $\frac{1}{6}$ so it becomes clear that the chance of ones turning up on both throws is $\frac{1}{6} \times \frac{1}{6} = \frac{1}{36}$. We can postulate the law,

The probability of two events A and B occurring is the product of the probability of event A and the probability of event B.

This definition is not really satisfactory because, while it covers the simple example of dice, it does not adequately define events A and B and under other circumstances it may not fit the case.

So for a second example we will take a pack of playing cards and look at the chance of drawing two aces from the pack on consecutive draws (we do not replace the first card before drawing the second). There are four aces in fifty-two cards, so our chance of drawing an ace first time is $\frac{4}{52} = \frac{1}{13}$. For our second draw, there are only three aces left in the pack so the probability of drawing one of them is $\frac{3}{51} = \frac{1}{17}$ and the overall probability of drawing two aces is $\frac{1}{13} \times \frac{1}{17} = \frac{1}{221}$.

It will be seen that the probability of an ace on the second draw is dependent on the outcome of the first draw. We have a condition attached to it and it is accordingly called the conditional probability.

We give a conditional probability a notation of the form $P(B \mid A)$, which means the probability of event B given that A has already happened. The symbol comes *after* the stroke defining the condition necessary before the probability applied. We will now re-write our law of chance, and say

If the probability of event A happening is $P(A)$ and the conditional probability that event B happens, given that event A has already happened, is $P(B \mid A)$, then the joint probability of both events A and B happening is $P(A) \times P(B \mid A)$.

This law is called the product law, and can be written $P(A \text{ and } B) = P(A)P(B \mid A)$.

We will now start again, with another example using dice. Suppose that in one throw we want to know the chance of getting a one or a two. The chance of a one or the chance of a two is $\frac{1}{6}$. So it will be clear that the chance of getting either is

$$\frac{1}{6} + \frac{1}{6} = \frac{1}{3}.$$

We can start to formulate our second law of chance by saying that the probability of either event A or B is the probability of event A + the probability of event B.

Again this is an unsatisfactory definition because it does not describe the events sufficiently. In the case of the dice example it is quite impossible for a one and a two to occur together, but in other events this may not be so.

Returning to our playing cards, suppose we consider the probability of drawing either an ace or a spade. We could draw the ace of spades, so the two events could happen together.

This brings us to the term *mutually exclusive*, meaning that the events cannot occur together. In the dice example we had mutually exclusive events, but in the card example we did not.

Clearly, where the events are not mutually exclusive, some allowance must be made for this fact. We have already seen that the probability of two events occurring together is the product of the probabilities of these events and the adjustment required is to subtract this product from the sum of the probabilities. The reason for this can be easily understood by reference to Fig. 15.7, which shows the probabilities set out in the form of areas.

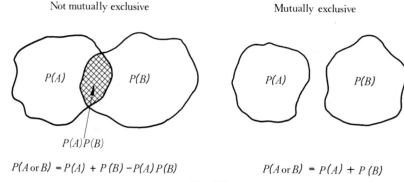

Not mutually exclusive Mutually exclusive

$P(A \text{ or } B) = P(A) + P(B) - P(A)P(B)$ $P(A \text{ or } B) = P(A) + P(B)$

Fig. 15.7

This method of approach enables us to find a simple solution to the case where we have more than two probabilities that are not mutually exclusive, and the diagram for three possible events A, B, and C is set out in Fig. 15.8.

$$P(A \text{ or } B \text{ or } C) = P(A) + P(B) + P(C) - P(A)P(B) - P(A)P(C) - P(B)P(C) + P(A)P(B)P(C)$$

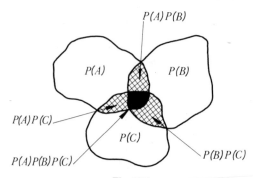

Fig. 15.8

174

Notice that the last term is added because, as the diagram shows, this area has already been subtracted three times in the previous terms.

We are now in a position to write the addition law of chance, and for simplicity will restrict it to two events.

If events A and B are alternative possible outcomes and are mutually exclusive, and the probability that event A happens is $P(A)$ and that event B happens is $P(B)$, then the probability that either event A or event B happens is $P(A) + P(B)$.

If events A and B are not mutually exclusive, the probability that either event A or event B happens is $P(A) + P(B) - P(A)P(B)$.

In reliability, we seldom find cases where failures are mutually exclusive, and the first part of this law is of little interest to us.

Armed with these laws of chance, we are now in a position to consider the outcome of a number of events, and the events we are interested in are survivals and failures. Where we are concerned with the occurrence of a number of failures, we will use the product law, and where we want to know the probability of one of a number of possible failures occurring, we will use the addition law.

The product rule If we look at the product law in terms of reliabilities, which are probabilities of survival, we see that where a number of items are concerned, the probability of all of them surviving is the product of the individual probabilities.

Since each probability concerns survival, it will be appreciated that conditional probabilities need not be taken into account, these are more likely to arise where we are concerned with probabilities of failure.

We can write:

$$R_E = R_1 R_2 R_3 \cdots R_N,$$

where R_E is the reliability of the equipment, and R_1, R_2, R_3, ..., R_N are the reliabilities of the N items of which the equipment is composed.

This is known as the *product rule*, which expressed in words is:

The overall reliability of a system is the product of the reliability of all the individual components that go to make up the system.

We have already used the product rule to build up mortality curves. We calculated the probability of failure before a given lifetime by taking the product of the probabilities of survival during increments of this lifetime. Similarly, we can break down a mortality curve to obtain the probability of failure during a stated period, given that survival has been achieved to the beginning of the period.

For example, suppose a boy has survived to the age of 10 and we want to

175

know the probability of his survival to the age of 20. We divide the probability of his reaching 20 by the probability of his reaching 10. In mathematical terms we write:

$$R(20 \mid 10) = \frac{R(20)}{R(10)},$$

$R(20 \mid 10)$ meaning the probability of reaching a life of 20, given that a life of 10 has already been reached.

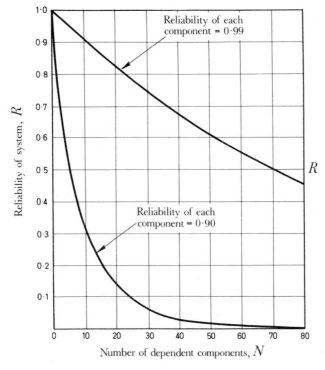

Fig. 15.9

The product rule is one of the most important rules in engineering reliability. It was first put forward by Robert Lusser and is sometimes referred to as Lusser's rule. Lusser was concerned with the production of V1's during the second world war. He noted that an unmanned aircraft had the disadvantage, compared with a manned one, that if any failure occurred during flight there was no human agency to attempt to overcome the effects of the failure. Any failure was accordingly fatal to the delivery of the bomb. Realizing that success depended on the product of the reliabilities of all the individual components of the V1, he set about improving these in order to produce an acceptable overall reliability.

176

The way in which the reliability of a complex system decreases with the number of unreliable components in the system is illustrated in Fig. 15.9, which refers to a hypothetical case in which all the unreliable components have a reliability value of 0·99 and 0·90, that is, they are expected to fail once in 100 times or once in 10 times during the relevant period. The figure shows the overall reliability of the system plotted against the number of components that are unreliable. It is a plot of 0.99^N and 0.90^N against N. It will be seen that the overall reliability decreases very sharply as more unreliable components are introduced.

As another example of the effect of the product rule we will take the case of a modern strike aircraft, which inevitably has a large amount of complex equipment packed into a very small space. A high degree of reliability is essential, since the time at which the aircraft delivers its attack is important. An advancing army does not wish to wait while its supporting aircraft have defects rectified.

Let us suppose that our hypothetical aircraft has the reliabilities shown in Table 15.6 so far as a single mission is concerned, that is, the probability that the particular system will perform satisfactorily for the duration of the mission. Taken independently, each system appears reasonably reliable, but the product of these reliabilities gives a figure of 0·95. In other words, out of every hundred aircraft ordered to attack the enemy, five will fail to get there simply because of their unreliability.

Table 15.6

System	Reliability
Airframe	0·998
Engines	0·994
Engine starting	0·993
Navigation system	0·990
Weapons system	0·994
Communications	0·982
Controls	0·998

We are also in a position to calculate the effect that the elimination of any particular cause of failure will have on the overall reliability of a system. The values of the unreliabilities of the different systems associated with our strike aircraft are shown in the form of a histogram in Fig. 15.10 in order of value. Eliminating the failures in the communications system would have the effect of improving the overall reliability from 0·95 to 0·967, a worthwhile gain, while working on the failures of the control system could, at the most, improve the reliability to 0·952.

The principle of attacking the main sources of unreliability in order to produce the maximum gain is termed the Pareto principle, after its propounder. When the reliabilities of a system or large piece of equipment are set out in the manner shown in Fig. 15.10, it will very often be found that attention to a few areas will bring the unreliability down to a reasonable level, while, from the point of view of the overall reliability, rectification of a large number of lesser causes of failure would have no marked effect. Dr Juran has called it the vital few and the trivial many.

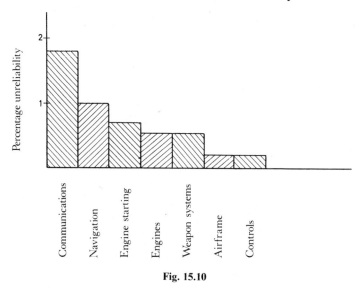

Fig. 15.10

Redundancy We will now apply the product law of chance to unreliability. In the case of a two-engined aircraft, we may be concerned with the chance of both engines failing in the same flight. If the probability of each engine failing is F, then the probability of both engines failing is, by the product law, F^2, ignoring the conditional probabilities that may be associated with this particular example.

This is a case of redundancy: the failure of one engine does not cause failure of the aircraft, so that one engine can be regarded as redundant. Since the probability of both engines failing is clearly very much less than the chance of one failing, F^2 as opposed to F, a two-engined aircraft is that much safer than a single-engined one.

Where we have redundancy we can write

$$F_E = F_1 F_2 \cdots F_N,$$

where F_E is the unreliability of the equipment, and F_1, F_2, ..., F_N are the unreliabilities of N items of which $N - 1$ can fail without causing the equipment to fail. In terms of reliability, this becomes

$$(1 - R_E) = (1 - R_1)(1 - R_2)\cdots(1 - R_N).$$

178

Stating this in words, we have

The unreliability of a system composed of redundant components is the product of the unreliabilities of these components.

The simplest way to introduce redundancy is by putting components in parallel. For example, if we want to make sure that the failure of a light bulb does not plunge us into darkness we can put two bulbs in parallel, or, for increased certainty, three. Then if the unreliability of a light bulb is F, the probability of having no light is F^2 or F^3.

Components can be put in parallel in two ways. They can be permanently connected in parallel, as we could do with our light bulbs, so that they were always both lit. This is called *active redundancy*. Alternatively, stand-by components can be brought into use following an initial failure. Our light bulbs could have separate switches so that when one went out we switched the second one on. This is called *stand-by redundancy*.

From the point of view of reliability, both systems can have advantages. In the stand-by system, there is less chance of the stand-by component wearing out or otherwise degrading, because it is not in continuous use. On the other hand, some switching mechanism is required, either manual or automatic, and this in itself may be unreliable.

Planning of tests

The chance of being able to test the absolute level of reliability of a piece of equipment is remote, for this is a luxury that can seldom be afforded. The Poisson chart (Fig. 6.8) shows this in a quantitative manner. Suppose that 100 samples of a component can be made available for test, and that it is required to demonstrate by test that the reliability of these components is 98 per cent. On the average, 2 failures are to be expected from the sample of 100 components. The Poisson chart shows that there is a 33 per cent chance of 3 or more failures occurring during the test of 100 components. In simple terms, even though the equipment is in fact 98 per cent reliable, 1 in 3 times when testing 100 components the obvious conclusion is that the reliability is at best 97 per cent. Either the results must be presented only with confidence levels shown, or no attempt should be made to show the absolute levels of reliability by test.

Tests are much more worthwhile when being planned to prove the unreliability of a particular component in a piece of equipment. The test programme must be specifically designed to find not the absolute levels of unreliability, but which features are the least reliable. These features can be improved in the correct order of priority, and hence the absolute level of reliability improved. Some degree of overstressing must be applied during these unreliability tests if answers are to be provided in a reasonable time scale. Overstress should be interpreted in a liberal fashion, and not taken to mean that only the normally applied loadings should be increased above the design conditions. Other factors which may influence reliability should be increased to provide a degree of overstress:

(a) The components should not be given any special selection or treatment
(b) The surface finish can be degraded to the minimum that would normally pass inspection (this may be different from the minimum that is specified on the drawing)
(c) Applied electrical voltages or hydraulic pressures can include a degree of fluctation on the nominal values applied
(d) Handling damage can be added, especially if fatigue failure is the likely mode of failure
(e) Over- or under-lubrication
(f) Omit some of the securing bolts to increase vibration levels
(g) Misalign the equipment.

There are many more.

All this is with a view to showing what will fail first, and what therefore requires improvement. The result will not be quantifiable in the form of 'Now the reliability is 90·2 per cent', but they will be quantifiable in the form 'The unreliability has been halved and the mean time between failures doubled'.

The test plan in this case is straightforward. The equipment is tested with such overstress parameters as the engineers consider to be appropriate until the first failure occurs. The minimum repair is effected, and the test continued unabated in order to find the second most important cause of unreliability, and the third, and the fourth. If nothing at all breaks or deteriorates, then the test is not a success, but a complete and utter failure. Something must be made to fail in order that the potential weaknesses can be located. From the times to failure it may be judged how many of the problems are worth curing, and which can be left as being satisfactory. If things are satisfactory, they should not be 'improved' for this may introduce new sources of unreliability.

Often it is desired to test alternative configurations, alternative designs, the product from alternative suppliers, alternative methods of manufacture, or alternative materials. This is where pre-planning the test programme can be so very valuable, and the factorial method and variants on the factorial method may be adopted. Let us consider first the simplest case, in which there are only two alternatives, X and Y. It is required to determine the effect on reliability (or performance) of changes in X and changes in Y. The classical scientific approach is as follows:

(a) Hold X constant and investigate the effect of changes in Y, and repeat the test to confirm the findings
(b) Hold Y constant and investigate the effect of changes in X, and repeat the test to confirm the findings.

That is, test 1 $X = X1$ test 2 $X = X1$
              $Y = Y1$ $Y = Y1$

   test 3 $X = X1$ test 4 $X = X1$
            $Y = Y2$ $Y = Y2$

   test 5 $X = X2$ test 6 $X = X2$
            $Y = Y1$ $Y = Y1$

A much more economical test programme arises when the test is pro-
grammed as follows:

	$X1$	$X2$
$Y1$	a	b
$Y2$	c	d

This matrix shows four tests only, $X1Y1$, $X2Y1$, $X1Y2$, $X2Y2$ with
test results a, b, c, d.

To determine the effect of X, we examine and compare $(a + c)/2$ and
$(b + d)/2$.

To determine the effect of Y we examine and compare $(a + b)/2$ and
$(c + d)/2$.

It will be seen that all four tests are being used to examine the effect of
changes in X, and all four tests are being used to examine the effect of
changes in Y. The testing is therefore very efficient and economical. But
there is more than that, for it is possible with factorial testing to examine the
effect of interactions. In an interaction, X and Y together are producing
changes different from those changes that would be expected due to a
change in X alone plus a change in Y alone. An interaction is taking place if
the results a, b, c, d plot out as in Fig. 15.11.

Factorial testing can be used for any number of variables, but since the
number of tests required for a full factorial test is 2^n, where n is the number

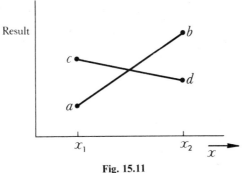

Fig. 15.11

181

of variables, there is a practical limit to the number of variables that can be examined in this way. If there are four variables W, X, Y, Z, then the test programme would be laid out as follows:

		X1		X2	
		W1	W2	W1	W2
Z1	Y1				
	Y2				
Z2	Y1				
	Y2				

If the relationships are non-linear over the range being examined, then it will be necessary to test at more than two levels of the variable. The test programme for X and Y, where relationships are non-linear, may be laid out as follows:

	X1	X2	X3
Y1			
Y2			
Y3			

Where many variables are operative, it will be necessary to reduce the number, either by using engineering judgement or by combining variables into groups and examining the effects of those groups. The more significant of the groups may then be examined in greater detail by factorial testing within those significant groups of variables. This grouping does mean that the number of interactions that can be studied is reduced. An hour or two laying out test programmes in this way can often produce the optimum test programme and result in more efficient tests that are both quicker in producing results, and cost less money to carry out.

In deciding which variables to include in the tests, or even before that stage is reached, when deciding which components to test, it is necessary to decide which components or variables are the vital or critical few, and which are the trivial many. The vital few are those components which control the reliability of the complete product, for it is invariably only a few items which persist in failing frequently. Items which fail very rarely are often best left, since it would take too long to prove whether an improvement has taken place or not. And by that time, probably nobody cares anyway.

The vital few can be isolated by test in the manner described above, by testing equipment until something breaks, carrying out the minimum repair work, and then carrying on until the next item fails. Another way of selecting the vital few for special attention is by a careful examination of service data, to find out those items which have a history of being causes of unreliability. Such an analysis produces quantitative information on the causes of unreliability, and will typically produce a picture such as that in Fig. 15.12.

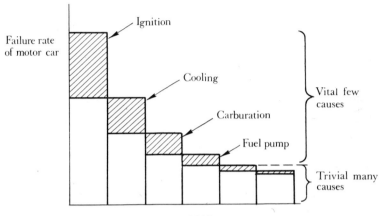

Fig. 15.12

β-life concepts

The β-life concept is of particular importance in the bearing industry, since there it is of especial interest to consider the life before a particular percentage fail. Large populations are involved in general when the subject is bearings, and to use time to first failure as a criterion would result in very conservative designs of mechanical equipment using bearings. Equally well, to talk about average lifetimes is not often acceptable or constructive, since the simple-minded customer is not really interested in having half of his equipment with failed bearings. He might well in the interests of economy consider having 5 or 10 per cent fail before he makes the effort to replace all the bearings. The bearing manufacturers therefore normally talk about β-10 lives, which simply means the life by which 10 per cent of the total population will have failed. Similarly, β-5 is the life by which 5 per cent will have failed, and β-20 is the life by which 20 per cent will have failed.

The β-10 life of a particular product has different values depending on the sample size tested, since the larger the sample tested, the smaller the variability will be. One can of course put confidence limits on the estimation of the β-life, and state for example that the β-10 life is 11,500 hours at the 95 per cent confidence level. This would mean that on the basis of the tests carried out, there is a 95 per cent chance that the β-10 life will not be less than 11,500 hours. If 11,500 hours is reasonably satisfactory, then most engineers will take the 5 per cent chance that the true answer is a little less than that.

In determining the β-10 life it is not necessarily essential to test until 10 per cent of the population has actually failed. If the test results are plotted on Weibull probability paper, for example, the results of the first few tests may be conveniently extrapolated to determine the time by which 10 per cent of the total population will have failed. This is illustrated in Fig. 15.13.

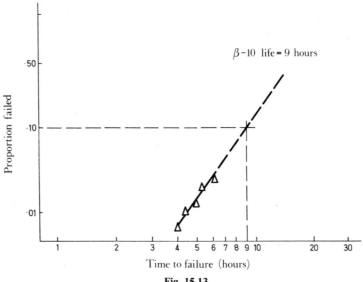

Fig. 15.13

The effect of maintenance

We must now consider the effect that maintenance has on mortality curves. Maintenance, in this context, refers to all inspection, repair, or replacement procedures that are carried out to prevent failures occurring. Where failures are prevented by maintenance, such maintenance will be a prime factor influencing the form of the mortality curve.

The situation is illustrated diagrammatically in Fig. 15.14, in which a mortality curve that would occur if there were no maintenance is modified to produce the mortality curve actually experienced. I_1, I_2, etc. are the times at which maintenance takes place, and A_1, A_2, etc. are the periods during which a degree of degradation, not apparent on inspection, develops to the point of failure—for example, the time between a crack just being undetectable and its causing failure.

Maintenance may include an operation that nullifies the effect of previous degradation, for example a fatigue-damaged layer of material may

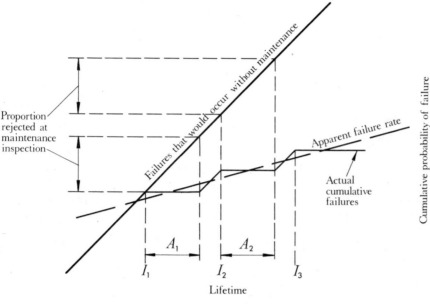

Fig. 15.14

be removed. It may also include a repair procedure that affects the subsequent rate of degradation. Accordingly A_1, A_2, etc. cannot always be taken as equal.

It will be readily appreciated that, after the first maintenance inspection, the actual mortality curve can be used to estimate future failures, provided there is no change in maintenance policy, but it is of no value for providing other information about the failures.

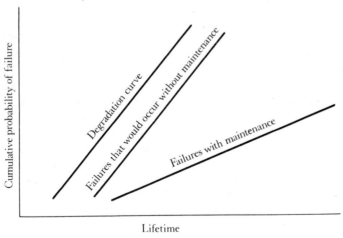

Fig. 15.15

Where the mortality curve ceases to be of much value, the degradation curve takes over, so that we always have one curve available for describing either the degradation or failures with respect to the total life of a part.

A diagrammatic representation of the various curves is shown in Fig. 15.15. This figure includes a line showing the mortality curve that would be expected if no maintenance were carried out. While such a curve can only be estimated it is an interesting exercise to do so, as it describes the true reliability of the design. Up to the time of the last failure that occurs prior to the first maintenance, the true mortality curve can be drawn, and the distance between this and the degradation curve represents the average time between the particular level of degradation described by this curve and failure. If the degradation curve represents the occurrence of detectable cracks, we can determine the average time that the crack takes to propagate to failure, but not, unfortunately, anything about the variation in this time.

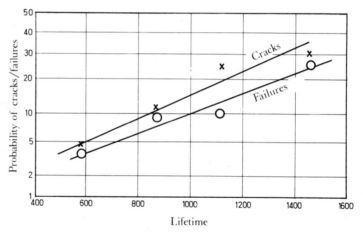

Fig. 15.16   Example of degradation and mortality curves of compressor blades

An example of a degradation and mortality curve up to the first maintenance inspection is shown in Fig. 15.16. This relates to the cracking and failure of compressor blades in an aircraft axial-turbine engine. In most cases, the failures were found on maintenance inspection, and the mortality curve has been calculated using the same procedure as for a degradation curve. Both curves are sensibly normal, as is to be expected when a large number of parts are equally exposed to failure, and are shown on normal probability paper. It will be seen that they are approximately parallel, the distance between them being the average time between the crack becoming detectable and failure occurring.

16

Making the best use of early-failure experience. Pointers from one, two, or three failures

We have studied mortality and degradation curves and the way these can be used to provide information. Unless these curves are drawn to describe the results of tests to failure they only come into existence because we have failures, a state of affairs we wish to avoid. We should also like to be able to find the best decision regarding action to be taken before we have had enough failures to be able to draw a mortality curve.

When one or two failures occur whose consequence can be serious or costly, questions must inevitably be asked about the number to be expected in future, and the life at which the failures will start to occur. Let it be said at once that analysis of the data is unlikely to lead to any conclusions that are not apparent from engineering judgement and a quick look at the data. Where the items that fail are among those with the longest lives, there is virtually no useful analysis that can be done, but where there is some good experience beyond the times to failure, it can be useful to support engineering judgement by such an analysis. At the best, given sufficient data, analysis can only set boundaries to what may be expected to happen, and these boundaries are inevitably of a very crude nature.

We will explore what we can do by means of an example, in which the data, though limited, is sufficient for boundaries to be set and some rough pointers obtained to future failures.

The example relates to cases of bearing failure in an aircraft engine and the available data is set out in Table 16.1. We will consider the data relative to the first failure. The probability of failure at 835 hours is $\frac{1}{24} = 4.15$ per cent, and we can plot this point on a piece of Weibull paper as in Fig. 16.1. We have considerable good experience beyond 835 hours, and clearly we wish to use this.

A good method of approach is to estimate the upper confidence curve. We read off the confidence limits for $n = 1$, $N = 24$ from the chart. The points are plotted in Fig. 16.1. We now wish to bring in the subsequent good experience where no failures have occurred. Taking the situation at 993

187

Table 16.1

Lifetime	Exposure	Proportion of failure	F(t)	Upper confidence limit 90 per cent
First failure				
835	24	1	4·15 per cent	12*
993	20	$\frac{20}{24} = 0\cdot83$		13
1298	18	$\frac{18}{24} = 0\cdot75$		13·5
1440	15	$\frac{15}{24} = 0\cdot62$		14·7
1691	10	$\frac{10}{24} = 0\cdot42$		18†
2046	8	$\frac{8}{24} = 0\cdot33$		20·5
2503	5	$\frac{5}{24} = 0\cdot21$		26
Second failure				
1172	19	$1 + \frac{19}{19} = 2$	9·20 per cent‡	21·5
1440	15	$0\cdot62 + \frac{15}{19} = 1\cdot41$		23·5
1691	10	$0\cdot42 + \frac{10}{19} = 0\cdot95$		27·5
2046	8	$0\cdot33 + \frac{8}{19} = 0\cdot75$		32·5
2503	5	$0\cdot21 + \frac{5}{19} = 0\cdot47$		

* Average number of failures = 1. From Poisson chart (Fig. 14.5), there is a 90 per cent probability of 2·8 failures. This is equivalent to 2·8/24 = 12 per cent.

† Average number of failures = 10/24 = 0·42. From Poisson chart (Fig. 14.5), there is a 90 per cent probability of 1·8 failures. This is equivalent to 1·8/10 = 18 per cent.

‡ See text.

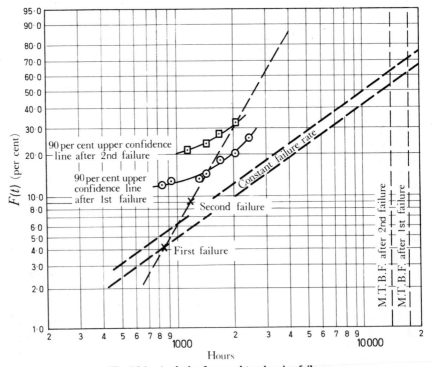

Fig. 16.1 Analysis of one and two bearing failures

hours, we have had 20 exposed. We can say that of these we have had $\frac{20}{24} = \frac{5}{6}$ of a failure previously, i.e., we have $N = 20$, $n = \frac{5}{6}$. The probability associated with this statement is 4·15 per cent, as previously, but our confidence has changed. By interpolating, we can read the upper confidence limit off the chart in Fig. 6.8. The upper confidence limits obtained in this way are shown tabulated in Table 16.1, and the line has been plotted in Fig. 16.1.

In the instance we are using as an example, a second failure occurred almost immediately after the first, this being at 1172 hours, the exposure at this life being 19. The exposure at the time of the second failure was little different from that at the first, and for the purpose of our example we will regard it as the same.

We proceed in exactly the same way as for the first failure:

$$F(1172) = 1 - 0.9585(1 - \tfrac{1}{19}) = 1 - 0.9080 = 0.092.$$

The tabulation for the upper confidence limit is given in Table 16.1, and the result has again been plotted in Fig. 16.1. We will study this figure and see what it tells us.

Taking the first failure and its associated upper confidence limit, we see at once that there is a pointer that the failure rate may be something like constant. It is clearly unlikely to increase appreciably with lifetime, particularly when it is remembered that the upper confidence line shown is a function of the size of the sample exposed to failure and accordingly may well slope more than the true upper confidence line.

Now, taking the second failure, we have a second upper confidence line. This does not mean that the first confidence line was wrong; there was after all a 10 per cent chance of points falling above it. It may be noted that the second failure point is well inside the original confidence limits, and the two failures, occurring so close together in calendar time, are clearly tending towards an extreme case. We can draw a line through the two failure points and this shows a considerable failure/time relationship. However, even if we assume the confidence line associated with the second failure to be correct, we can be reasonably sure that no such failure/time relationship exists. Something approaching a constant failure rate still appears likely. In fact, the failure referred to in this example is identical with that shown in Fig. 10.10, which has a slightly increasing failure rate with lifetime ($\beta = 1.2$).

From this example, we see the dangers of attempting to estimate a failure/time relationship from a sample of two, and also that a comparatively small amount of good experience at times subsequent to failure can provide a good indication of the upper boundary of this relationship.

The example also illustrates what can be done when we have a small number of failures—one, two, or three. With five, we can draw an estimated mortality curve, and four is an intermediate number at which we

189

might be able to draw a mortality curve depending on the number exposed to failure.

Comparison of demonstrated reliabilities

It is often useful to produce a simple comparison of the *demonstrated* reliabilities of the various components that go to make up a piece of equipment, particularly during the development or early service stage in the equipment's life. To this end, we can plot on one sheet of paper the points that arise from all the failure modes experienced by the particular equipment. Besides being useful for comparison purposes, such a plot is helpful in enabling a quick assessment of the achieved reliability to be made.

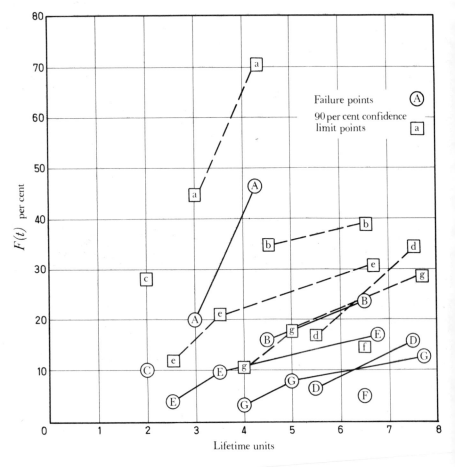

Fig. 16.2 **Hypothetical plot of demonstrated $F(t)$-values**

The plot can be done on the basis of

(a) the actual failure points,
(b) the upper confidence line,
(c) both (a) and (b).

A hypothetical example of a plot that shows both the failure points and the upper confidence bands is shown in Fig. 16.2. Each failure mode has been given a letter for identification.

A plot of this nature can be used to assist in the allocation of priorities for corrective action. It is unlikely that such priorities will be decided on the basis of expected numbers of failures alone; cost or severity must be taken into account. It is a simple matter to replot Fig. 16.2 on the basis of cost. The cost of each failure is estimated and multiplied by the probability values for each failure mode. The result is values of probable cost. Using probable cost as the vertical scale, the data can then be re-plotted.

Prediction of the reliability of equipment at an early stage

It is often desirable to make a prediction of the reliability of equipment at a relatively early stage in its life, for example at the time of initial entry into service. This can be done by calculating the M.T.B.F., as revealed by proto-type experience for all the failure modes that have not been eliminated by redesign, and while such a procedure is simple to apply, it takes no account of lifetime relationships, and cannot be regarded as satisfactory. There is also the question of the adequacy of the changes that have been made to eliminate failures. Cases will arise where there will be insufficient ex-perience of the change to demonstrate that it is an effective cure.

It is inevitable that any early prediction that is made must contain a fair measure of engineering judgement, since if sufficient failures of any indi-vidual mode have occurred to enable an accurate analysis and prediction to be made the proportion failing is likely to be so high that corrective action will have received priority.

A good method of approach is to start with a map of demonstrated relia-bility such as those shown in Fig. 16.2, and using judgement to predict the mortality curves for each failure mode, taking account of the engineering parameters involved, the type of failure, and previous experience of the mortality curves that particular types of failure produce. For example, quality faults will be given a curve showing a falling failure rate, and wear-out failures a rising rate. In cases of doubt it may be sensible to assume a constant failure rate for a period. Where there is doubt about a cure being effective, the failure can be retained and its mortality curve included. Figure 10.3 shows the hypothetical treatment of the demonstrated relia-bilities (at 50 per cent confidence) given in Fig. 16.2, it being considered that failure modes A, B and C have been eliminated. This plot has been done on

Weibull paper, which can make the prediction of the probable mortality curve easier.

Once the mortality curve for each individual failure mode has been predicted, it is a simple matter to work out $F(t)$ for the whole equipment, using the product rule. Such a curve is shown in Fig. 16.3. This may be an underestimate of the actual reliability that will be experienced because additional failure modes may manifest themselves as life proceeds and the number of pieces of equipment exposed to failure increases. Again, engineering judgement coupled with past experience must be used to estimate the probable increase in unreliability.

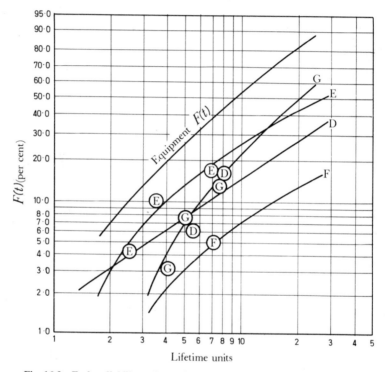

Fig. 16.3 Early reliability estimate from experience and engineering judgement

17

Is reliability a saleable commodity?

Yes and no. It all depends on the type of industry you are in. In the aerospace industry one can give an unqualified yes. Considering the technical complexity of their missions, the reliability achieved by the Apollo space missions is remarkable. One hundred per cent safe returns of the Apollo astronauts at the time of writing must be the reliability success story of the second half of the twentieth century. Did someone say why? Simply because reliability was written into the specification along with other performance parameters at the conceptual stage of the project. Tenders were therefore on the basis of achieving the standard of reliability written into the specification.

Go to London Heathrow Airport, or Chicago O'Hare, or New York Kennedy, or Paris Orly, or Los Angeles International and ask any traveller what he thinks about reliability. Huge flying machines of 300 tons and more, powered by motors developing 20,000 or 30,000 or 40,000 horsepower each, in a package some 2m diameter × 4m length, are expected to be ready to go at the precise time specified in the timetable written many months before. Perhaps only the engineer can marvel at this fantastic achievement; the ordinary traveller simply wants his aeroplane to leave on time, or else he will fly with another airline.

Go to Paris or Milan and watch the motor cars revving up their motors at the traffic lights, waiting for the green light to signal the next racing start. Each of those motor cars has in series piston, bearing, connecting rod, bearing, crankshaft, coupling, clutch plate, clutch-withdrawal bearing, clutch, train of gears, propeller shaft, differential gears, etc., and no driver gives a moment's thought to the possibility that his car will not leap forward at that green light. If it does fail he is half way to buying a different make of car.

At the other end of the scale if your ball pen costing 3p fails to operate, I suspect that you pick up another one and carry on. At that price and technical complexity there is not the same expectancy of a completely trouble-free operation.

In a free economy, the incentive to strive for a high level of reliability is simply one of profit. In each market situation, the individual firm or organization must assess the level of reliability necessary to enable the required sales targets to be achieved, along with the other engineering parameters of performance and operating characteristics. The production costs that must be maintained to enable the product to be put on the market at a competitive selling price will usually dictate the type of construction to be employed. Where this is novel, then the engineering development costs must allow for the spending associated with achieving the required level of reliability. Launching a new product which has an unsatisfactory reliability can make a complete nonsense of the best-laid marketing plans. The development work can, in many cases, be used as part of the marketing strategy, and can form an essential part of the launch programme. It is also good insurance if the initial reliability is shown in the specification, for the customer is usually much less irate if he believes that the trouble has struck in spite of a sensible and visible programme of work designed to check out the reliability of the product.

Examples of the combined development and marketing strategy come from the motor industry, the gas-turbine industry, and the fan industry. When a new model of car is announced it produces two opposite reactions in the potential customer's mind:

(a) it is new (and therefore 'better' than the previous one)
(b) it is new (and therefore unproven and potentially full of teething troubles that will give unreliable operation)

The strategy is to make the customer think it is new (and therefore better than the previous one and therefore desirable) and it has been well proven by test (and therefore should have few hidden faults which will require frequent visits to the service station). To do this it is vital to include in the publicity the more readily understood tests to prove the reliability of the new car, such as 'this car has been driven for 100,000 miles before we let the public know of its existence', or 'two hundred selected motorists have been given this car to test to make sure that our new car will stand up to the rigours of everyday business motoring'. Both of these examples have been used in the past to try and involve the motoring public in the extensive development work that has been carried out on their behalf to arrive at a desirable and reliable product.

The strategy in the aero-engine industry is similar in that there must be a convincing reply to the airline or armed-forces customer who says that he can remember the teething troubles he had with the last new engine, and what has been done to make sure that he does not have to go through a similar period all over again? The simplest way to put over the development programme is to show that with the previous new engine, 10,000 hours of engine running were carried out on the test bed before entering airline or military service, but with the new engine, 14,000 hours of running will be carried out on the test stand before service operation begins. The

194

financial implications of this are great. In this sort of situation it is absolutely essential to use the very best market intelligence about what the customer really wants, and is really prepared to pay for.

In the fan industry the customer is concerned with price, performance, and reliability, and usually in that order. There is therefore likely to be less money in the kitty for elaborate testing, and every test must be meaningful to the engineer and convincing to the customer that he can install the product and forget it. Field testing is therefore very important for it is relatively cheap, but of course takes a fair amount of elapsed time. The customer here is particularly convinced by seeing installations, or details of installations, where the new product is running satisfactorily. Damp, steamy, or dirty installations are particularly desirable to introduce an element of 'overstress' testing into the field service trials.

If the fan is to be installed in an agricultural situation, then it is important not to field test the fans with the most careful user that can be found, but rather with one who cleans down in a more haphazard fashion, hosing down the equipment when he should not, and being a bit lax about when he or she changes the filters. The hosing down may well show that a flinger needs to be incorporated on the shaft to stop water entering the motor and ruining the reliability.

But when all that has been mentioned in this book has been taken into account, and the product is reasonably reliable, it must also look business-like and reliable. A reliability engineer with a large motor manufacturer carried out an interesting survey of owner-driver reactions to the reliability of their vehicles. The drivers of the large angular cumbersome looking model were full of complaints about their cars, and seemed upset by quite minor faults. On the other hand, the drivers of the new fast-back which had been introduced by the same manufacturer and was still suffering from teething troubles was not subject to the same criticism—'Trouble? no, not much. The gearbox did have to be changed after 500 miles and the paint is all falling off, but nothing much really'. Just because the product looked good and looked reliable. Volkswagen with their beetle car which sells on its reliability may well be the exception to prove the rule that not only must it be good, it must also look good.

Index

active redundancy, 166, 170, 179
addition law, 167, 175
aircraft engine, 113
airports, 193
alternative configurations, 180
Anderson, 133
Apollo, 193
apparent failure rate, 156
asymptote, 61
average, 43

ball-bearing, 131, 132, 134
ball pen, 193
bathtub curve, 142
bearing failures, 188
bearing separator, 131, 132
bearing track, 130, 140
beta, 60, 61
beta-life, 183
bi-modal distribution, 100, 103, 143, 144, 146
binomial, 59
    distribution, 67, 68, 69, 73, 76
block diagram, 165
Brook, 100, 103
burn-in, 11

cards, 41
central limit, 41
    theorem, 86
chance, 41, 172, 173
chi-squared, 159–64
Christmas tree lights, 70
Cicci, 104
coin tossing, 75
component rejection, 152
compressor:
    blades, 118, 142
    discs, 106
confidence:
    double-sided, 77
    limits, 75, 76, 78, 81, 84, 162, 187
    single-sided, 77
constant-use condition, 111

corrosion, 28, 104, 116
cost of failure, 13, 157
crack:
    formation, 35, 37, 51
    propagation, 51
creep, 29, 30, 57, 119, 120, 144
    resistant, 54
    steel, 109
critical few, 182
cumulative distribution function, 47, 59, 60
customer use, 121
cycles-to-failure, 99

damage, 104
data, 47
datum parameter, 61
death, 4
degradation, 37, 55, 103, 150–8, 184, 186
degrading mechanism, 30, 32
demonstrated reliability, 190
detector, 71
deterioration, 108
deviation, 43, 45
dice, 172
dispersion, 90
distribution:
    skew, 10
    symmetrical, 10
distributions, 9, 29, 30, 40
dominant variable, 119
double-sided limits, 162
duty, 27–31, 121, 123, 128, 140
    distribution, 111, 113
dynamic strength, 128

e, 25
early-failures, 187
economic life, 12
elastic strain, 99, 103
Ellison, 100
endurance limit, 110
engineering considerations, 117

Epstein, 164
eta, 60, 61
exclusivity, 75
experimental error, 98
exponential distribution, 24
exposure, 17, 55
extrapolation, 107
extreme value distribution, 85, 88, 90, 92, 98, 119

factorial testing, 181
failure, 2, 27, 30, 37, 55, 65
failure:
  distribution, 85
  rate, 6, 7, 38
    constant, 11, 12, 23
    local, 7
fatigue, 28–30, 40, 54, 139
  failure, 116
  life, 113
  tests, 99
frequencies, 160

gamma, 60, 61, 65
  estimation of, 65
gears, 142
gear-teeth, 128, 129
Gumbel, 90

hardness, 40
hazard rate, 7
histogram, 4, 42, 45

imperfections, 100
inclusions, 106
increment, 43
initial strength, 139
inspection, 139, 184
interactions, 122
iterative methods, 79

Juran, 178

lambda λ, 24
latent period, 61
Lewis Research Centre, 133
life, 31, 32
  to failure, 95
lifeband, 151, 153, 154
log double exponential, 96
log:
  extreme value distribution, 85, 95, 106

normal distribution, 40, 51, 52, 54, 56, 57, 61, 103, 106
long-term fatigue, 103
lowest values, 93
Lusser, 176

maintainability, 158
median, 9, 10
  rank, 20, 79
minimum life, 99, 104
mission reliability, 2
mixed distributions, 143–9
mode, 9, 10, 97
money, 158
Monte Carlo, 121
mortality:
  curve, 4, 11, 14, 47, 49, 81, 82, 84, 87, 150
  force of, 7
motor car, 193, 195
multinomial distribution, 70
multiple items, 165–86
mutually exclusive, 174

negative exponential, 73, 92, 101, 119
nimonic alloy, 104
non-destructive testing, 39
normal:
  distribution, 40, 41, 42, 46, 47, 51, 61, 86, 92, 98, 112, 114
  duty distribution, 117
  probability, 47, 48, 49, 50
notches, 104

parallel components, 165
Pareto, 177
Parker, 133
Pascal's triangle, 69
peak values, 113
plastic strain, 99, 103
playing cards, 173
points of weakness, 85
Poisson, 159, 162, 179, 188
  distribution, 59, 71, 73, 79
prediction, 12
probability, 2, 173
  distribution function (PDF), 4, 25, 43, 45, 56, 57, 138
  of being greater/less than, 91
  of failure, 67
  of surviving, 67
product rule, 18, 165, 170, 175
proportion, 14, 20

198

quality, 105, 136, 142, 143, 147
  control, 39

random, 101
  selections, 121
range, 45
rank, 49
  order number, 20
  values, 79
ranking, 18
Rayleigh, 114, 115
real life, 151
redundancy, 168, 178
Reichard, 133
reliability, 1, 2, 67
  curves, 3
repair, 185
replacement, 150–8
return period, 90
Rockwell hardness, 133
roller-bearing, 131
rolling contact, 131, 142
Rolls-Royce, 103

safety, 157
  factor, 38, 39
sample, 42
scale parameter, 60
scatter, 87, 107, 108
  factor, 123–5, 133
scientific approach, 180
series components, 165
service data, 183
shape parameter, 60
short-term fatigue, 103
Simonds, 164
simple systems, 165–86
single-sided, 119, 163
skew, 112, 119, 131
skewness, 90
stainless steel, 139
standard deviation, 44, 45, 47
standby, 79
redundancy, 170, 179
strain range, 99

strength, 27, 30, 35, 46, 47, 58, 85, 100,
  109, 121
  distribution, 24, 49, 87, 94
  initial, 85
stress concentration, 111
structure, 40
surface finish, 40
survival, 2, 96, 176
  curve, 3
symmetry, 42

tail, 61, 102
tensile test, 49
test:
  plan, 180
  planning, 179
  programme, 121
  results, 100
thermal shock, 113
time-dependent failure, 131
time-to-failure, 19, 121
true elastic limit, 33, 53, 55
turbine:
  blades, 57, 86, 118, 144, 155
  discs, 85, 88, 98

unreliability, 2
usage, 112

variable, 46, 47, 59
variability, 13, 14, 136
vital few, 182
Volkswagen, 195

warning system, 70
weakness, 46
weak spots, 100, 103, 136–42
wear, 28
wear-out, 11, 12
Weibull, 58, 59, 62, 63, 64, 87, 90, 96,
  123–5, 128, 131, 140, 146, 184, 192

Yates' continuity, 162

Zaretsky, 133

MADE AND PRINTED IN GREAT BRITAIN BY
WILLIAM CLOWES & SONS, LIMITED, LONDON, BECCLES AND COLCHESTER